He Spoke. I Listened.

Dear Mary Jane,
May you
always feel His
nearness & remember
He can do anything.
Love,
Diana Stuhr

To order additional copies, please contact us.
BookSurge, LLC
www.booksurge.com
1-866-308-6235
orders@booksurge.com

He Spoke. I Listened.

Diana Stuhr

2006

He Spoke. I Listened.

TABLE OF CONTENTS

ACKNOWLEDGEMENTS:

The author gratefully acknowledges the editors who volunteered their time and expertise. The finished product is finer because of you: Doris Chalfant, Darnell Knauss, Donna Stacy, Hannah Hurley, Emily King, Amy Stephens and Chris Stuart. Thank you!

Bert Beuoy and Betty Moore, thank you for consistently cheering me on to the finish line.

Darline Hammer, thank you for generously providing along the way to make this dream become a reality. It couldn't have happened without your help.

Mackenzie Phillips, thank you for sharing your art. Please keep on drawing and painting.

Bekka Siggelkoe: thank you for sharing your spectacular photographs. Your partnership in this project brought me much joy. To purchase or view in color or black and white these or other photos by Bekka, you may contact her at (bsiggelkoe@gmail.com).

Cover photo: Diana Stuhr, author.

For my sisters who regularly make me laugh until I can't breathe (WMP). Our story of separation and reunion could be another book.

INTRODUCTION

Over the years, people on my partnership team encouraged me to write a book. I've always shrugged my shoulders at such suggestions believing the dream of becoming an author was beyond my reach. I also felt the world was full enough of verbiage and everything that needed to be said had already been said. However, I eventually realized with the freshness of a spring rain that I, being made uniquely, yet in God's image must use the gifts God has given me. God speaks through my uniqueness uniquely.

The words He speaks through me to the world, He's never spoken before in just this way.

"A word
Uniquely wrapped
In flesh.
A gift
Like none other
Given over and over
FRESH
In every child born."

Bekka Siggelkoe

LISTENING

This is a place for writing, for listening,
A place of attentive silence,
Where I sit expectant.
With patience, pen poised
I wait for you, Oh God
To speak.
I wait-hopeful
The silence will scatter like leaves in the wind
At the sound of Your voice.
I wait with longing,
Wondering if my self-absorption distorts the sound
Or blocks it out entirely,
So that
All I hear is me.
I wait-certain that there are things You want to say
Through me to the world.
If I could but see
As I wait for You,
You're waiting also for me
To be ready to hear You clearly and with understanding.
Since I was in Your mind
Then in Your hands
While I was being knitted together,
You formed words You'd say to me
Only
And so You wait for me
Unhurriedly.
Let the silence now be broken, Lord.

Please speak Your word to me
Uniquely.
With pen poised
I'm ready, O God for you to speak.

UNFINISHED

Unfinished

I saw it today in my angry friend firing off words
in machine gun like fashion; hurtful words intended to
wound.

Unfinished

I saw it today in the one who took each verbal bullet
blow on a heart already scarred and still bloodied from
the last battle.

Unfinished

I saw it today in one who cradled close to her, as she
might a helpless babe, a bundle of bitterness she loved too
much to abandon.

Unfinished

I saw it today in the tear-streaked faces of a couple
who had tried everything and yet again they grieved the
not yet shaped, eagerly anticipated and longed for little
one who lay between them on a bloodied towel crushing
hope in them.

Unfinished

I saw it today in one whose face became contorted at the very image of their enemy-a colleague they would not forgive. "Oh, no, this one must pay for what he did to me", said with poisonous venom that filled even me with dread.

Unfinished

I saw it today in a parent overcome by the willfulness of a child deaf to the plea that they obey. The helpless parent shrugged in surrender and let the willful child have his way.

Unfinished

I saw it today in a spouse betrayed and still in shock uncertain how it happened that the parting came before the death. It mattered not for something in them had died. Each tomorrow would only be a walking death anyway.

Unfinished

I saw it today in a tattooed teenager whose heart was as pierced as her face. Not with smooth and gleaming wires but with barbed and blackened ones. The chip on her shoulder had grown wall like barring anyone who dared to get close to her.

Unfinished

I saw it today in the elderly saint bent over in her chair with wheels, who can no longer go where she wishes or do what she wants. Though her mind is sharp, arthritis has so crippled the tent in which she resides helpless and waiting. She awaits the shedding of this flesh for a resurrected body whole again.

I'm reminded of the cry of Jesus from the cross, "It is finished." All our unfinished-ness can be brought to Him, the Finisher. What a comfort to know that He who began a good work in us will complete it. Like Him, we'll cry one day, "It is finished." All our unfinished-ness will be forever gone.

***

SOMETIMES

Sometimes you have to break the law to get close to Christ like the hemorrhaging woman did. The law said to touch Him would be a crime.

Sometimes you have to raise eyebrows and risk embarrassment to get close to Christ like the perfume anointer did. The sinner and the righteous should never mix together or so the righteous said.

Sometimes you have to cry out persistently to get close to Christ calling attention to yourself though others shush you harshly, like the blind man by the road did. Those not blind prefer not to see you. If only you'd keep quiet they wouldn't have to.

Sometimes you have to step out of the crowd to get close to Christ like the leper who came back to say thank you for his healing.

Sometimes you have to stop working and sit quietly to get close to Christ though it may make others mad at you for shirking your duties, like Mary did.

Sometimes you have to risk danger to get close to Christ like the woman at the well did.

Sometimes in order to get close to Christ you have to be carried there by friends like the paralytic.

I wonder about the hemorrhaging women who held back because they couldn't face one more failed attempt to get well and therefore died in their uncleanness.

I wonder about the potential perfume anointers who spent their valuable asset on themselves unwilling to risk the exposure of a Christ encounter.

I wonder about the blind men who allowed those with sight to quiet them, assenting that it is best for them to not be seen.

I wonder about the outcasts who remain untouched, lost in a crowd of untouchables, immersed in anonymity because obscurity is safe.

I wonder about the workaholics who condemn the apparent "laziness" of colleagues believing that by their works they shall be saved.

I wonder about the women alone who never ventured near the well while a solitary man sat on its rim for fear that he would hurt them like all the other men they'd ever known.

I wonder about the paralytics without friends who care enough to carry them or even to tear a roof apart if need be.

For each who came to Christ, there were many who did not. It's about taking risks believing He is God. It's about not giving anyone else a Godlike place in our lives directing how we should act and what we should do. It's about shedding anonymity to hear Him call our name. It's about trust.

***

JUST THE BACK OF HER HEAD

I met him at a dinner theater. He was 13. He'd come with his grandmother who was legally blind. I watched his gentle care of her and wanted to learn more about him. It turns out his grandmother had raised him from a baby. I asked him if he knew his mom or saw her sometimes. He looked me square in the eye and said without emotion, "I have one picture of my mother." There was a pregnant pause and then he added matter-of-factly, "It's the back of her head."

I was speechless, initially unable to form a response to this emotionally packed phrase. Then I thought of Jesus who knows what it feels like to have the last picture of the one you love to be only the back of their head. It was on the cross God, the Father turned His face away from Christ and forsook Him.

It comforts me, Lord that you understand the depth and scope of this boy's buried pain. Tonight his story connected me in a fresh way to your experience on the cross when your Abba turned away leaving you with your last human memory of Him to be the back of His head. Help me, Lord to find the words I need to connect this boy to the truth that you understand His pain in ways that I cannot.

***

AN EVER PRESENT HELP

I met with Ellen as I usually do on Friday noon time. Little did we know as we enjoyed lunch together how different life would be for her in just a few short hours. Without warning, she was thrust into a nightmare that was Job-like. (Interestingly, she had just finished reading through the book of Job). The burglary of her home and the theft of everything and anything of value produced a numbness that enshrouded her like a heavy cloak of fog. I entered the fog with her and experienced a little of the numbness, but most of all I desired to help us not lose sight of Jesus in the ensuing darkness.

Each day as the nightmare ebbed and flowed, I found the Word reverberating with a constant theme, "I am with you," like blinking neon signs flashing through the darkness repeatedly. "The Lord is good, a refuge in times of trouble...He pursues His foes into darkness" (Nahum 1); "When you pass through the waters, I will be with you" (Isaiah 43:2); and "The Lord your God is in your midst, a victorious warrior" (Zephaniah 3:17) were some of the verses illuminating the darkness. Not to mention the Psalms that point again and again to God's ever-present help.

The nightmare continues traumatizing and tiring in its totality. Jesus knows the way through this hard-to-navigate night. We follow closely for we know we'd be lost without Him. Thankfully, He holds tight to our hands.

***

GOD HAS NEVER FAILED ME

The Lord promises a future, a hope-filled future; but today my future is unclear. What's ahead is hidden as if in a thick fog. There are options, of course, just like when I longed for marriage in my younger years, there were always options, but none that seemed exactly right or good. Not having a visible future is scary. I find the fog frightening. The "what ifs" loom large.

But this one thing I know: **GOD HAS NEVER FAILED ME.**

His Word to me today is wait. Don't interfere with what I have planned. Only what I've planned will have my blessing, He tells me. I ponder the possibilities like a child anxious to open a wrapped gift. I get restless in the waiting. I nag, "Is it this? Is it this?" Did I say I find waiting hard? I do.

Today I have food on my table and a roof over my head and I am grateful. A future, a hope-filled future is mine, as I wait on Him. He promised it. I need steadfastness in the waiting and reminders of the truth that: **GOD HAS NEVER FAILED ME.**

***

PAINFUL MEMORIES

It was an unexpectedly emotional moment. Remembering sometimes is. It happened at a girl gathering.

Suddenly I was transported to a kitchen in St. Paul Minnesota, to the home of a dear elderly nurse (Miss Garnett) where I and my friend, Mary, were renting a bedroom just after graduation from nurse's training. Miss Garnett had learned of our plan to wrap my then boyfriend Bruce's car in toilet paper and had requested we not do it. On the day I was remembering we had just returned home from defying her. We assumed she was at work. Over cups of coffee in her kitchen, we loudly rehearsed our toilet papering escapade, which escalated into slanderous remarks about Miss Garnett. We called her names like "old fuddy duddy."

I'll never forget the moment our laughter was effectively silenced by the appearance on the stairs of Miss Garnett in her nightgown. Not only did I want to take back every slanderous remark, I also wished I hadn't defied her. It was a painful experience for all of us. I loved Miss Garnett and I had hurt her deeply.

At this weekend's girl gathering, I hurt again for wounds I'd once inflicted on someone else and tears welled up at the memory.

Together the girls and I coined a new phrase. From now on, if we remember, we'll call slanderous comments "Miss Garnetts" and when we hear each other making such remarks all we'll have to say is "Miss Garnett." Some memories, though painful, are worth recalling.

***

IT'S A GIFT

It is a gift to wait while the one you are with tries to form the words that express matters of the heart.

It is a gift to sit quietly with them, embracing the silence, until the wordless groanings break into the stillness, capped by sobs erupting from a heart with cavities never before entered but suddenly opened.

It is a gift to allow your tears to fall unheeded to mingle with theirs as together you journey over wounds freshly formed. It is a gift to bring with you the healing salve of understanding and love.

It is a gift to provide covering for a heart laid bare before you in order to shelter its exposure.

It is a gift to love wordlessly, carefully, honestly.

Who will receive this gift from you today?

***

LIFE IS PRECIOUS

My friend began his story with the simple words, "My wife and I went shopping this week." Turns out they were buying funeral clothes for three children ages 2-9. Their 29 year old mother, my friend's niece, was dead. She had shot herself and it was these same, soon to be funeral-clad, children who had found her. This mother left an unspoken message her children will always remember. Her action said, "When things get hard, give up; when life becomes overwhelming, throw in the towel."

Left are three small children who will never forget they weren't reason enough for their mom to hang on to life. Talk about abandonment.

Gone forever is this mother's chance to cheer at ballgames, help with schoolwork, watch and coach through childhood crushes, fix hair for prom night, stand proudly at graduation, give counsel for college choices, buy mom-of-the-bride wedding attire, and hold grandbabies.

Reflecting on the story, I cried for three small children I've never met and a mom who gave up on herself and them.

***

LIFE FOLLOWS DEATH ALWAYS

Fall is my favorite time of year, that is, until spring sprouts new life; then I get really excited. Last year in August I was pondering how we color death black, but God paints it red, yellow, orange and brown.

Today I sat in the woods and watched as the wind violently shook the trees around me and the leaves danced their death descent. It was both terrible and beautiful. The trees were slowly being stripped of their leaves so recently green with summer life. I wanted to turn away from their partial nakedness, for as I sat there, I realized that I, too, have experienced a stripping away in this season of death to false assumptions and inadequate, inappropriate coping mechanisms. There is vulnerability in this, a process of dying. There is, also, the promise of fresh life, transformation and new growth.

I shuffled my feet and kicked up the dying leaves scattered about the forest floor. I marveled that God doesn't vacuum up these leaves and re-attach them to the trees again come spring. He doesn't recycle dead things like I do. I'm thankful that He doesn't and today I told Him so.

I left the woods grateful He's birthing new things in me, like the way I view myself, my world and others. I left the woods determined to welcome needful deaths, which lead to fuller life. I left the woods anticipating spring, but not wanting to rush its arrival.

Fall is my favorite time of year, at least for today. May fall days remind you life follows death-always.

***

DEATH

We color death black
God paints it yellow, orange and red
We cling to life not wanting to let go
Not wanting to be dead.
The leaves let loose the tree
Because they know
Spring can't follow snow
Without their letting go.
They fall to the ground in colorful array.
Their death dance is sometimes vibrant, sometimes slow.
We color death back and wish it wasn't so
God paints death with rainbow hues to show
Life follows death.
Don't you know, better is the letting go?

**

A MOVIE THAT MOVED ME

I went with friends to see the movie SECONDHAND LIONS Saturday. My emotions were stirred many times during the movie; most deeply, perhaps, by the issue of abandonment.

I was particularly moved when the boy's mother sends him off alone with her abusive boyfriend. Out of sight of the mother, this man hits the boy hard in the gut in an effort to intimidate him. The boy fights back, but is no match for the man. The boy's lion hears the struggle and comes charging from the cornfield. (You'll have to see the movie to understand how the boy comes to have a pet lion.) The lion pounces on the man and saves the boy but dies in the process of a probable heart attack. (Note: I'm not telling you what happened to the man.) As the boy holds the dead lion, tears streaming down his face, he says to his uncles, "He looks like he's smiling." The uncles answered that he died happy protecting his cub.

Ironically, unlike his mother, the lion recognized an enemy, knew the child was in danger and acted to defend and protect the child. I saw myself in the boy and realized with profound thankfulness that God provided people in my life who were like that lion. They protected, loved and defended me and were there for me when my Mom wasn't and should have been. And they continue to be there for me. The insights from this movie made me once again grateful to God for His provision at critical junctures in my life journey.

In a later scene in the movie, the mother makes the statement, "I don't have a choice...," to which the boy replied, "Maybe YOU don't . . .." It was the moment he realized he didn't have to be as helpless as she was choosing to be and that realization changed the direction he was heading. He captured the moment and acted with courage. It was a clarifying moment, a decisive moment, a moment for taking charge. It changed him.

May you not miss the life-changing moments stuffed with opportunities that come your way. And when you identify them, may you realize you have choices, too.

Diana Stuhr

STOLEN SEEDS

It happened when I was staying with my good friends, Ronnie and Mary. He had lingered that morning to make me coffee before heading off to work, where a steel plate fell several feet hitting him in the head, leaving him unconscious, and placing him in the neurological ICU attached to lots of tubes. I had a picture standing there at his bedside of a bird I once watched in the Philippines. The bird was rolling a seed down a slanted roof and just before it rolled off the edge, he'd swoop down and catch it, fly back to the top and roll it down again. Suddenly, out of nowhere, a bigger bird swooped in and stole the seed. I was instantly angry. How dare that bird interfere with the game, I fumed. I watched the little bird sit still for a long time and then it flew away returning almost immediately with another seed which it rolled down the roof.

Life is like that. A steel plate falls and the routines of living are interrupted and forever changed. What was is stolen, gone forever; for we cannot remain as we were no matter what the outcome.

This is the sitting still time. The time of anger, anguish and tears. The time to let it all sink in. But sometime in the future, the routines of living will resume though they may not be the same. It will be a different seed. Ronnie heated my cup while the coffee brewed before he left for work, before the big bird swooped in. Now we cast ourselves on God's mercy as we wait to see what God will do for our beloved Ronnie in ICU.

***

TRIBUTE TO A FRIEND

I learned yesterday that my friend and colleague was tragically killed in a car accident. When I think of her, I picture calm in a sea of churning waters. She was the eye of the storm, unruffled and unhurried, though very busy and rarely still. Her six children rise up and call her blessed. They were obedient and well-mannered children with hearts she molded and shaped as she modeled "what is required of thee, oh man, but to do justice, to love mercy and to walk humbly with your God." That was her.

She had a clear picture of right and wrong and the determination to right as many wrongs as possible. She made time for me when her time was limited and could have been spent a thousand other ways. We laughed over coffee and cried over shared hurts. We joined our hands and hearts to pray worries away.

I visited her in the town where she home schooled her children and helped her husband with the translation of the New Testament. I saw her juggle the needs of her husband, her children, her neighbors, and her guests. She bubbled over with ideas she implemented. Worldly wealth mattered little to her. Missionary kids (she was one) mattered more. It was one of her passions to offer an anchor to missionary kids, who felt adrift in a sea of uncertainty as graduation from high school loomed just ahead of them.

She wasn't perfect, but she was godly. Her house wasn't tidy like mine. She didn't do things the way I might do them, but she loved me and I loved her.

She was a listener, a talker, a lover of people. She was my friend.

Today I'm grieving, but not as one who is without hope.

***

IMAGELESS

Imageless. It's what I am when someone is indifferent to me, when I don't factor in on their radar screen. It's when someone doesn't care if I fly right or if I crash and burn. There is nothing noteworthy about me to like or dislike. They'd be hard pressed to describe or identify me. I am nothing to them. When you are invisible, people can't see you. When you are imageless they can see you, but they don't bother. You're not worth the effort of forming the features that make you, you. You just are but they couldn't care less. It's a terrible feeling to desperately want one someone to see you and know they never will no matter what you do. And when that someone is your father or your mother, the little girl in you grows up slowly finding it hard to see herself as she really is. Her features are formed over time by significant others she learns to trust who do see her and reflect to her what they see. She bears scars from her imageless years; some she'll carry with her until the Image Maker calls her to Himself. New scars may form over old ones if she allows it. The indifferent ones may keep wounding her if she lets them. She must learn to tell herself the truth:

1. She doesn't need to let anyone hurt her anymore.
2. She doesn't need to let the indifferent ones define for her who she is.
3. She is not imageless. She bears the image of the One who made her. By looking to Him, she'll

find herself reflected in His eyes and realize who she really is. He shouts for joy because of her. She is the apple of His eye. He loves her responsively. She will never be imageless to Him.

Slowly it is becoming enough that He sees her, even when others choose not to.

***

LIFE LESSONS

Life lessons learned in my sister's kitchen. It all began with a recipe I found in a magazine. It captured my attention and I suggested we make it.

We set out for the supermarket to gather the necessary supplies to make the "best onion rings ever." Thankfully, my mathematically-challenged brain cells never trouble me with realistic details like how much it's going to cost to make each onion ring versus how much it would cost to buy a ready-made order of onion rings from a nearby restaurant. This detail did not escape the notice of my nephew, Jason, however, who watched us unload said supplies.

Life lesson number one: Best always (according to some) to compare the cost of making it from scratch versus buying the finished product.

Thankfully my nephew didn't stick around to watch the ensuing fiasco. The batter didn't stick to the onion rings when dropped in the saucepan of grease. Floating batter and limp onion rings did not endear me to the recipe. I was ready to throw in the towel, dump the batter in the nearest garbage pail and call in an order for onion rings from the nearby restaurant. My sister, the cheerleader, was not willing for me to do that just yet. She stood beside me encouraging me to keep dipping and dropping and would you believe, the batter finally stuck and we began pulling out onion rings that looked like they'd been made in the finest restaurant around. Tasted like it, too.

Life lesson number two: Don't take on a project that might fail without making sure there is a cheerleader on the team who won't let you give up prematurely.

Life lesson number three: It helps to have the proper equipment lined up before you undertake a task. Substitutions don't always work as well as the real thing. We learned the grease wasn't hot enough for the first few attempts and the saucepan just wasn't cut out to be a deep fat fryer.

We finally enjoyed the homemade onion rings, but Jason's got a point. It did cost us more than an order of onion rings from the restaurant would have cost us, but you know what? You can't put a price tag on the value of life lessons learned in the kitchen. I wouldn't trade in those memory-making moments of chalking up a life experience whatever the cost.

***

SHARING A HEARTBREAK

I went to court this past week with my friend whose son faced the Judge. During the hearing, he kept begging for a second chance having completely lost count of all the second chances he's compiled over the past few years. I watched the proceedings with a heavy heart and then wrote this when I got home.

Dear child, I remember a time when you still fit in the kitchen sink and I was bathing you there one of the nights I babysat you. When your bath was done, I pulled the plug and we both watched the water swirl down the sink hole. Suddenly with utter terror in your eyes, you grabbed my arm tightly and exclaimed, "I'm going down the drain." Your words made me laugh then as I pulled you to the safety of my arms.

Today, sitting in the courtroom, I saw a much bigger sink hole and you swirling rapidly toward it, but I didn't see the terror in your eyes or any effort on your part to grab tightly to the arms held out to you for rescue.

Today I saw you, now a young man, truly going down the drain and it made me cry.

***

THE PIANIST

I was deeply moved by several things from the movie, "Pianist." It is a movie about the Holocaust during WWII. The opportunity to see the movie seemed timely because it just so happens I am currently reading a book called, "Hiding from Love."

I watched the survivor in the movie go from one hiding place to another in an effort to hide from evil. I decided hiding from evil often isolates us from love as well. Therefore, I have to ask myself if the value of hiding (which in our survivor's case was safety) is worth the cost of relationship; for it is in relationship that we learn to love. However, it is in relationship that we also learn to hate.

There were good and bad people depicted on the screen and my emotional response to each, as I defined them, was strong. But I've been pondering also the demonstrated goodness in the "bad" people. Does one act of kindness negate all the acts of evil? Jesus said that sin is sin. So who was good, really?

I'm told William Cameron Townsend, the founder of Wycliffe Bible Translators, often said that it is important to be kind to the least obviously significant people we meet day-by-day, for janitors become Presidents. I watched that truth depicted in the movie when the survivor's life is dependent on a radio technician he had seen daily in the studio where he played the piano before the war. A man whose name he never bothered to learn.

I was convicted earlier this year when I realized one day that I rarely note the people who serve me at the checkout line, at the post office, or in the coffee shop. Ten minutes after leaving them, if you had put them in a lineup, I wouldn't be able to pick out the one who had just served me. I in no way connected with them as humans. Now, I am making a disciplined effort to note these individuals, to call them by name when I can, to look into their eyes, to pray privately for them, to connect one human being to another.

Near the end of the movie a German soldier extended his coat to the survivor (the Jew in hiding). It reminded me of Jesus' words about giving your cloak. The marvel to me is that the offered coat was received. I know individuals who would rather die from cold than wear the coat of the enemy. I know of people who, every day, refuse the robe of righteousness Jesus offers. It is the covering with which we enter heaven. They would rather cling to their pride and go to hell. The survivor in the movie didn't let pride and a lack of forgiveness stand in the path of life for him. He conquered them as he buttoned the coat in place.

However, that coat nearly cost him his life when Russian liberators mistook him for a German. When they asked him, "Why the coat?" He replied, "I'm cold."

Simple truth. Why the robe of righteousness? I'm a sinner. Our survivor knew he was Polish and he was cold. I know I am a sinner and I need a Savior. Thank you, Jesus, for the robe of righteousness. I gladly put it on.

***

JOSEPH

I've been thinking about Joseph. As a youth, he had a dream from God in which he was the star. (Genesis 37:5-11) Imagine with me the horrific blow to his pride and his dream, when years later, he finds himself tied behind a camel as a slave bound for Egypt. (Genesis 37:28) Few slaves make stardom. Yet God was with Joseph and He made him successful *as a slave*. He rose to the highest slave place in Potipher's house. Was this the stardom of his dreams? Imagine with me the confusion Joseph must have felt in his circumstances. Yet we know from the Scripture that he clung to God. (Genesis 39:9)

Falsely accused by Potipher's wife, Joseph's next stop on the journey to stardom is prison. Yet God made him successful there, too. (Genesis 39:20-23) We know that even here, Joseph clung to God. (Genesis 39:8). Two full years, it says in Genesis 41, after Joseph had successfully interpreted the butler's dream, he (the butler) remembered Joseph to Pharaoh. Only then did Joseph's childhood dream become a reality. Pharaoh promotes him to the highest position in his kingdom. Only with respect to the throne is Pharaoh greater than Joseph. (Genesis 41:40).

I suspect the journey was not as Joseph pictured it, but he never lost hope. He clung to God through every unwelcome and unwanted circumstance. How about you? On your journey to heaven, what camels have you followed taking you where you didn't want to go? How many temptations have you fled that only landed you in trouble falsely accused? How many lonely prison type places have you languished in with no guarantee of release?

Such experiences take the form of:
lost jobs,
lost relationships,
lost reputation,
lost social standing,
lost finances,
lost material possessions.

Jesus said, "If anyone would come after me, he must deny himself and take up his cross and follow me. For whoever wants to save his life will lose it, but whoever loses his life for me and for the gospel will save it. What good is it for a man to gain the whole world, yet forfeit his soul? Or what can a man give in exchange for his soul? Mark 7: 34-38.

***

GOD'S PAIN-FILLED HEART

I was reading in Genesis this week about Noah. I'd love to put my name in Genesis 6 verse 9 and have it be true of me, "Diana was a righteous woman, blameless among the people of her time and she walked with God." God's assessment of Noah's time went like this, "Man's wickedness was great and every inclination of the thoughts of his heart was only evil all the time. The Lord was grieved and His heart was filled with pain." (Genesis 6: 5 & 6) Today I considered the pain-filled heart of God in Noah's day and also how pain-filled His heart must be today.

We live in a wicked world full of violence just like Noah did. Chapter 9 verse 20 of Genesis indicates that Noah was a man of the soil, not a carpenter. Don't you love how that doesn't matter to God? It wasn't what Noah did, but who Noah was that made him God's man for boat builder. It wasn't his skill; it was the condition of his heart that made him God's pick. I must remember that.

Noah did everything just as God commanded. That's my challenge: to be obedient to the One whose heart is pained because of man's disobedience.

***

CHOICES

When reading once in Numbers 13 and 14, I imagined how a young girl might have viewed the happenings. This is about her.

The journey so far had been long and difficult. They were nearly home, or so it seemed. Caleb and Joshua confirmed that this was the place. The fruit they had brought from a forage there was undeniably enviable. The young girl listened silently to the debate about whether to go ahead and take the land or not as questions formed in her mind.

Were they to remain refugees or were they to become residents of a land richer than they had dared to imagine? That issue was even now being hotly debated. She could almost see the fear that settled on the crowd as the discussion reached a fever pitch.

To embark on a wilderness journey in order to get somewhere was one thing. But to choose to continue to wander in a wilderness aimlessly seemed absurd to her. Yet that was their choice wasn't it? She sighed as she helplessly watched the crowd turn against Caleb and Joshua. It was obvious from the discussion they weren't going anywhere. And so it came to be that Israel wandered another 40 years in the wilderness.

We're often not very different from the Israelites when it comes to obeying God, to believing He is able to do all that He promised. What's the journey been like for you these days? Are you wandering through a wilderness of your own choosing or are you partaking of the milk and honey morsels he's chosen for you?

I hope you're able to say without reservation or fear, "Yes, Lord, yes to your will and to your way." I hope the giants looming over your path don't cause you to turn back from His promises. I hope the Word hidden in your heart is lighting up the trail to your land of milk and honey.

***

SCAREDY CATS

God came. Moses noticed, but he didn't recognize it was God until He spoke from a burning bush that didn't burn up. I wonder how many bushes were set aflame before Moses noticed.

God spoke. Moses listened and questioned. Barefoot, feeling vulnerable and afraid of God, of the Egyptians, of his own people, Moses talked with God. Years ago he'd enjoyed the splendor of Pharaoh's court until. ... Perhaps "fugitive-at-large" posters still hung in public places bearing his more youthful image and detailing his terrible crime.

Surely God didn't mean for him to go back. Back to what he'd fled. He left so afraid and was fearful still. How could he go back?

God calls scaredy cats and gives them work to do. It's as simple as that. I would have written Moses off as undesirable, unusable, and unacceptable. I'm encouraged that God didn't. That gives me hope.

I'm watching out for a God encounter with eyes peeled and shoes at the ready. God calls scaredy cats into service. That encourages me for I am one.

***

RED SEA ENCOUNTERS

I'm pondering this morning the Red Sea experience from someone prone to fear (someone like me). This is what I tell God when I come to my Red Sea experiences:

God, I don't do trapped places with no escape route.
God, I don't do sea crossings between walls of menacing water.

The Red Sea experiences I encounter are those impossible places where there seems to be no way out. Sometimes I find myself smack in the middle of my "I don't do" places.

When God opens up the sea for me and I head across to the other side on dry land, I find Him there waiting for me with His arms outstretched. I fall into them safe.

Safe, what a picture. To feel safe. To be safe.

Swallowed up, not by cascading blankets of water or by a blood-thirsty army, but by the strong arms of a powerful Loving God.

In my trapped places, I'm learning to tell God, "You open a Red Sea for me and I'll come to you, despite my fears."

Bekka Siggelkoe

RAHAB

I've been spending time with Rahab the past few weeks. Her story is found in Joshua 2. I call her the wise woman of Jericho. She has fearless command of a situation fraught with danger and intrigue. She tells believable lies that send the king's men on a wild-goose chase; she outlines a strategy that preserves the lives of the two spies when they leave her house; and she negotiates the safety of her family in the face of certain annihilation. Wow! What a woman.

One part of the story that was niggling at me was the fact that Joshua sent the spies. I asked myself again and again why he would do that. He knew it was a failed strategy used by Moses. He knew God had told him they would conquer Jericho and He would instruct them how to do it. So why did he send the spies? And then one morning I had my answer. The spies were sent because there was a Rahab that needed to be rescued. Wow!

Rahab believed in the one true God on the basis of a forty-year-old story she'd been told about a dried up Red Sea. Hers was a believing faith that led to life. I'm like her except that I believe a story that's over two thousand years old about a crucified Christ that rose from the dead. God sent two spies to rescue her. He sent Jesus to rescue me. She tied a red cord to her window to signal her belief. I gave my heart to Jesus for cleansing and transformation to verify mine. Believing isn't enough. There's an action that follows belief that leads to life.

Don't you love how God never lets a Rahab go unrescued?

Bekka Siggelkoe

JOSHUA: ONE OF THE TWELVE

I've been thinking these days about Joshua. He was one of the 12 spies Moses sent to spy out the Promised Land. Only he and Caleb, a fellow spy, believed the Lord that He would give them the land regardless of the terrors or potential obstacles that lay in their path. However, their optimism was overruled by the ten other guys not so trusting in God's ability to keep His promises.

But this is where I hit the pause button on the story unfolding as I read it: "the little ones that you said would be taken captive...they will enter the land...but as for you turn around." Deut. 1:30&40. This was the beginning of forty years of going in circles in the desert, forty years of pointless purposeless meandering. It was crazy-making monotony. There was no arriving, building, settling, or fighting. It was like living out of a suitcase for the rest of their lives.

And this is the stunning part: obedient, faithful, believing Joshua was not spared the consequences of his disobedient, unfaithful, disbelieving friends. He wandered like the rest. Oh, he was rewarded eventually forty years later. His was a future reality that required obedience, faithfulness and belief because there were no guarantees it would happen, except God said so.

Perseverance and faithfulness are characteristics of two (Caleb included) disappointed fighting men who could have been bitter and angry. They turned around like all the rest, but they never turned their backs on God.

I'm wondering about the wanderings of Joshua. I'm wondering if I could have remained so faithful despite the unfairness of it all. I'm considering also the plight of fighting men (those who perished in the wilderness) wandering with nothing to fight for. Today I'm considering the choices that lead to life and death and the joys and miseries in-between.

***

ALTARS OF REMEMBRANCE

In Joshua 3 & 4, I meet the God of organized instruction who tells His people exactly what they are to do. "Follow the ark," then "you will know which way to go, since you have never been this way before." Don't we all want clear guidance and someone to show us the way especially when we are venturing into new territory? The God of Joshua is the same God we love. He still says, "Follow Me," then "you will know which way to go, since you have never been this way before."

I wonder at the courage of the Ark Carriers who stepped into the swollen Jordan River trusting that God would not let them be swept away and drowned. Had all of them witnessed the Red Sea miracle? I wonder. I marvel at their patience while they stood as the whole nation of Israel hurried by them. They stood as twelve appointed men chose stones from around their feet. They stood until all that God commanded was accomplished.

I wonder how long they stood. Did they wish they had been given the task of stone-gatherers instead? Did they envy those already on dry ground safe on the other side? What were their thoughts? What did they talk about, if anything? God did this, the passage says, so that all the people of the earth might know that the hand of the Lord is powerful. He did it so the Israelites might always fear Him. The gathered stones would be their reminder.

Today at the office, the women I work with met together for lunch in our dining area. We each came with our own stone and shared our remembrances of things that God had done for us. With our stones we built an altar and praised our powerful God who is to be rightly feared.

***

MADE IN HIS IMAGE

The Old Testament is filled with stories as captivating as movies: battle scenes, mystery, intrigue, and romance. They are stories that fascinate me.

Like the story in Joshua 9. The Israelites are well known in their region and their reputation sends shivers down the spines of some like the Gibeonites, who rather than prepare for a war they were convinced they couldn't win, prepared instead for a deception that might net them survival.

Their preparation was crafty and well thought out down to the finest details of clothes, sandals, bread, sacks and wine skins. They memorized their story and had it down pat. The Israelites bought their ruse, believed their lies and never bothered to inquire of the Lord who sees beyond sandals and bread.

It took only three days for the Israelites to learn they'd been duped. The leaders took heat from the whole assembly who grumbled against them. I can't help being thankful I wasn't on that leadership team.

I also can't help wondering what God's plan for the Gibeoinites would have been had Joshua inquired of Him before making a treaty with them. By their craftiness, the Gibeonites were allowed to live peacefully with the

Israelites. Was this God's original plan for them? I can't help wondering if God wasn't somehow pleased with their creative cleverness. They were, after all, made in His image, too.

***

HANNAH

I was touched as I read about one woman's battle
with infertility. She made a deal with God that if He
would give her a son, she would give him back to the
Lord all the days of his life. And God did it. In the course
of time, she gave birth to a son. And she did it. When he
was weaned (how old is that?) she took him to the temple
and gave him to the priest (who by the way was wicked
and evil).

A woman of her word, Hannah entrusted her son to
a drunken priest to raise. She wouldn't be the one to kiss
his scrapes and make them better or to touch the heart
wounds he would undoubtedly receive as he grew. He
wouldn't run to her with questions in the night. She'd
only see him once a year when she and her husband made
the long trek to the temple. Every year she took him a
coat, each stitch undoubtedly made with the longing to
see him again and a prayer that God would watch over
him.

Her son, Samuel, became a very influential prophet
in Israel. In I Samuel 3:19 I read, "The Lord was with
Samuel as he grew up." Hannah hadn't really entrusted
Samuel to Eli to raise. It only seemed so.

I have to wonder how it would have been for the
nation of Israel if Hannah had withheld her son. I have

to wonder how it would have been for me, if Mary, the mother of Jesus had withheld hers.

You can read Hannah's story in I Samuel chapters 1 and 2.

***

THE WISE WOMAN OF ABEL
Based on II Samuel 20:14-23

I wonder about the wise woman of Abel. Was she a married lady? Why did no one stop her from reaching the top of the wall? How did she manage to make herself heard above the noise of the battering of the enemy attempting to fell the city's wall? When she got their attention, why did they do what she said? Why didn't they ignore her or dismiss her? Why did Joab let her accuse him and why did he defend himself to her? Why did this woman have confidence that she could produce Sheba's head? Was she the only wise woman of Abel? Why did people listen to her?

This story fascinates me. When you visualize the scene in your mind and consider the people all huddled about in fear; when you imagine the noise of the enemy building the siege ramp and the men gathering arms and planning strategy in various cluster groups, you can't help but marvel at the courage of one woman.

Where was Sheba while all this was going on? Was he, with his men, joining Abel's inhabitants to fight in the defense of the city? How did the wise woman of Abel convince Sheba's "army" of followers to relinquish him to her?

Perhaps authority comes with Godly wisdom. When the wise woman of Abel spoke people listened and a city was saved. What if she had surrendered to fear? What if she had let her doubts get the best of her? I can think of many reasons why it would have been more prudent for her to remain mute. She couldn't have known when she mounted the wall what the outcome would be.

***

THE WISE WOMAN OF ABEL
(Part Two)

I'm still thinking about the wise woman of Abel. I can't help wondering what happened to her after the city was saved. I doubt there were many parades or banquets in her honor. Women had their place, after all, and I suspect it wasn't on top of the city wall talking "man" talk with the commander of an army.

Perhaps there were powerful men in leadership who were embarrassed by her. Perhaps there were women who were awed by her and a little frightened of her, too, or at the least uncomfortable around her. Perhaps this embarrassment and discomfort left her alienated and lonely. I think it's possible that this was a bittersweet victory for her.

I've had my own bittersweet victories. It's partly the memory of the pain of the bitter that outweighs the pleasure of the sweet that sometimes keeps me from mounting city walls or slinging down traitor's heads to a waiting army.

It is my need to be accepted and liked by others and my fear of the loneliness of being left out that usually keeps me from experiencing the satisfaction of doing the right thing, the courageous thing, and the needful thing. After all, I know my place and it's not on the wall talking "man" talk to the commander of an army. Or is it?

Letting go of stereotypes is part of the process of healing for me. My counselor terms it "breaking rules I live by." For now we're learning what the rules are that bind me and keep me from living freely as Jesus desires I would. In fact it was just for such freedom that for me He died.

What I like about this woman is that she wasn't just thinking of herself; she was thinking of the city. It wasn't all about her. She knew what the right thing to do was and she did it. That's freedom.

***

WE ARE NEVER LEFT OUT

Reading in I Samuel 16, I notice that David, the youngest son of Jesse is left out, uninvited, excluded from the sacrifice event with Samuel.

Among the invited ones, there was not the one that God had chosen. Puzzled Samuel asked if there were other sons. "There is one more," Jesse told Samuel. David on the bottom rung, lowest in the pecking order was absent, missing, unconsidered, tending sheep somewhere.

"Call him," Samuel said.

I'm humbled to realize that God knows where every left out shepherd is and He will fulfill His calling on their lives regardless of others' disregard for them. God, Himself, calls shepherds in from the field, away from the sheep when there are giants to kill and kings to dethrone.

In God's time and in God's way, some pastures lead to palaces and some palaces lead to pastures (Moses). We are never forgotten, left out, disregarded by Him. I find that comforting.

***

DAVID'S DAY-TIMER

I pondered a page from David's (as in King David of the Old Testament) weekly day timer. (See I Samuel 29 and 30.) The month-at-a-glance section revealed a heavy schedule of raids he participated in the previous month with his six hundred fighting men. The whole of his raiding party, including women and children, were living among foreigners (enemies of Israel even) in Philistine territory. It was a survival strategy to live there. It was a way of escape from King Saul's murderous attacks and it seemed to be working.

David and his men found themselves marching against Israel at the rear of the Philistine army. They were heading into a battle they did not want to fight. What could they do? How was God going to make a way of escape for them? The situation seemed impossible. David couldn't fight against his own people, nor could he let the Philistines know he was not loyal to them. Not a moment too late, God intervened and David and his men were sent home by the King because some of the other Philistine rulers distrusted them. What a blessed relief as they turned homeward; that is, until they came within sight of their city and saw the smoldering remains. God had intervened to solve one problem for David but within the same week he faced an even greater crisis. Every woman and child was gone.

David and his fighting men wept. There was not an unwounded man among them. The loss touched each one personally. Then in bitterness, the grief-stricken group turned on David but David turned to God-the God who rescues, the God who saves, the God who makes a way where there seems to be no way.

God instructed David to go ahead and pursue the Amalekites who had plundered them, so immediately they set off. When eventually they came upon the partying plunderers, a battle ensued lasting more than twenty-four hours. Miraculously when the dust of battle had settled, it became apparent David and his men had succeeded in restoring everything that had been taken. Can you picture the rejoicing as families were reunited? (Certainly the captured women had had little hope of being rescued. They knew their men were engaged elsewhere in battle. Despite their hopelessness and during it, God was executing their rescue.)

With jubilant joy on everyone's part, the trek homeward to Ziglag commenced. What a perfect ending to a perfectly horrid week, right? Wrong. There was a crisis looming just over the horizon. Another conflict brewing as the men who fought took their stand against the men who, too exhausted to fight, had stayed with the supplies. Again David, with the help of God, intervened to avert disaster.

Haven't you experienced similar weeks of highs and lows; times of crisis that seem to stack up one after another with little time for reflection in between? You just get one thing solved and another hits you.

David gained strength to manage the onslaught of trouble from God, the God who had proven He can rescue, He can save, He can make a way where there seems to be no way. Nothing is too difficult for Him. David knew that and so must we.

***

TWO PREGNANT ROOMMATES

I've been pondering the story of two pregnant roommates due almost on the same day. They had much in common. Neither one had a husband. Both lived the life of prostitution. Perhaps they didn't know who were the fathers of these little ones being knit together in their womb. Perhaps they'd shared the same partners. Perhaps they'd both schemed and dreamed of a future that would free them from the lives they were living. It seems they had no other children. Perhaps this was a first pregnancy for them.

Two women alone, sharing the pain of childbirth and then the joy of sons. Until one night one of the moms accidentally lies on her son and kills him. Imagine the horror, the grief, and the disbelief. There's no time for any of that for this quick thinking woman of action who trades her dead son for her roommates living one, while she remained asleep.

Can you imagine the climate of the household the following morning, the arguments that ensued at daybreak? Can you imagine the helplessness of the woman whose living son was now in the arms of an imposter, a woman not fit to have him, a woman with no heart? Feel her utter anguish and desperation!

She, too, is a woman of action who somehow gets an audience with the King. The baby trader is no match for this King. Wisely he learns who the real mother is.

You can read about these moms in II Kings 3:16-28. Two women prostitutes, two newborn sons (one living and one dead) and one wise King.

I think about the woman who accidentally killed her baby and my heart goes out to her. What a horrific tragedy. It can't be undone, though she tried to undo it. I wonder what became of this woman who seemed to lack remorse and compassion.

I think about roommates and companions on life's journey and the importance of choosing them wisely. I want my journey partners to be authentic people of integrity who admit their mistakes, who welcome others to share their burdens of grief and loss and who embrace difficult circumstances with the clear assurance that God is in control. I want my journey partners to be people of faith who point me to God step by step. I want to be that kind of journey partner for others who share the path with me.

***

A LITTLE CHILD SHALL LEAD THEM

I was receiving instructions for the gala Birthday Celebration for Jesus that Multnomah School of the Bible was hosting for the community. My fellow workers and I had gathered in the room already decorated for the reception that was to follow the program. There were balloons and colorful table decorations that had seemed common place to me until suddenly a four-year-old appeared in the doorway to the room. With his arms spread wide and grasping both door posts, his eye grew big as saucers at the decorations and he announced in a loud voice, "Hey, we're going to have a party!" The atmosphere in the room quickly became festive. Everyone smiled and some laughed out loud as the contagious enthusiasm of a four-year-old touched us all. It's party time everyone! Jesus is having a birthday! How special to see the event briefly through the eyes of this small boy.

It was equally amazing as I took my post across from the live nativity scene with a real baby and watched the children (especially the 3, 4, and 5-year-olds) approach the manger. For them this was baby Jesus and the reverence and awe clearly etched on their faces made me feel as though this really was Bethlehem. It was all I could do to refrain from removing my shoes and bowing to the baby so revered by little ones who hadn't yet grasped the difference between 2000 years ago and today.

Thank you, Jesus for this December night when you allowed me to see Christmas from the vantage point of pre-schoolers. I left the party changed because of them.

"A little child shall lead them." Isaiah 11:16

***

FEARLESS

In Isaiah 44 it says, "This is what the Lord says, He who made you, who formed you in the womb and who will help you, 'Do not be afraid.'" I pondered this simple directive from God in the light of conversations of recent days.

Confessions of fear fall easily from lips of friends concerned they would lose their jobs, their teen was running with the wrong crowd, their husband was rarely home, they had said the wrong thing, their paycheck wouldn't cover the bills, they couldn't accomplish the occupational tasks piling up around them, and they couldn't fulfill the expectations of family, friends, and supervisors. On and on expressed fears flitted about me like leaves blown by the wind.

Yet in my heart I know that as a child of God I should be fearless. In fact I realized anew that my Heavenly Father's peace must characterize me. It is one way I'm set apart as His child. It's one way I'm different from those who don't know Him personally.

Thankfully, He who made me, who formed me in the womb, will help me not be afraid. In a fearful world where anxieties accumulate, I look to the Prince of Peace to forge a pathway upon which I journey with Him peaceful and fearless.

Bekka Siggelkoe

COSTLIEST OF GARMENTS

Isaiah 61:10 says, "I delight greatly in the Lord, my soul rejoices in my God, for He has clothed me with the garments of salvation and arrayed me in a robe of righteousness." Reading it caused me to think of the time my friend, Gail and I visited the Nieman Marcus store in Dallas. We touched dresses that cost thousands of dollars each. I was in shock. I spoke to the sales clerk and asked the dumb question, "Do people actually buy these dresses?" It was beyond my comprehension that someone would pay such exorbitant prices for a garment.

Today I'm thinking about what the robes of righteousness cost my Savior. He purchased them for me with His blood. I'm stunned at the realization of the cost just like I was at Neiman Marcus. However, nothing in their stock compares with the garment my Lord bought for me. I'm arrayed in the costliest of garments, freely given.

***

RACHEL WEEPING FOR HER
CHILDREN

In my mind's eye, I visualized the little town
of Bethlehem around the time of Christ and let my
imagination wander as I thought about what it may have
been like for some of the women who lived in that town
then. I settled on one home after another and this is what
I imagined:

Finally, after so many months of being disappointed
again and again, Ruth held her long awaited and
beautifully designed boy close. She remembered distinctly
the day when she knew she had finally conceived. The
months of waiting while the baby grew had seemed to
go on forever. How fervently they had prayed for this
treasure, a gift from God that today stretched a smile
across her face from ear to ear. She spoke her love out
loud as he lay contentedly against her shoulder.

Martha cradled Timothy in her arms while a
shiver of fright coursed through her body. All her other
offspring one by one had died within their first year of
life. The disease was hereditary according to the doctor.
Still she hoped that this son might be spared the fate that
had befallen his siblings. Everyday she looked for signs of
the illness. In just a few more weeks she would no longer
have to worry. If Timothy survived his one-year birthday
without any sign of the disease it was most certain he did
not have it. She had hardly dared to hope, but Timothy

had already lived longer than any of the others. How she loved him. How she cherished the hours they cuddled. He was so alert and responsive. His laughter was like music to her ears. After so many tears shed at each previous death, she welcomed these sounds and encouraged them. Playfully he giggled as she held him in her lap.

Deborah squealed with delight. Matthew was trying again to stand. Nearly two now, he had been a source of joy every minute since his birth. His sisters, all five of them, adored him. Finally a boy was born to them. Her husband was so pleased. The stigma was erased. The women no longer whispered about her at the village well. Finally God had answered their prayers for a son. She didn't think she could bear another pregnancy. Thankfully, now, she didn't need to.

Leah felt her newborn's fingers tighten around hers and she gazed at him with wonder and love. She had never before held a baby of her own. Oh, she had been pregnant, plenty pregnant. She could no longer count the months of nausea spanning years of trying to birth a child. Each pregnancy had ended prematurely before life systems developed adequately. Each pregnancy grieved. Each leaving a hole carved in her heart that caused her constant pain for which there was no medicine. Today she barely felt the pain. Today she gazed into the eyes so like her own and dreamed new dreams for her son, for her husband, for herself. Finally they were family.

Suddenly sounds, terrifying in their harshness, pierced the morning's peace. Each woman paralyzed and confused looked towards the door of her home as soldiers burst through brandishing swords, seeking boys, small boys, all boys not yet three years old.

On a hill far away stood an old rugged cross upon which another mother's child would one day hang. But for Ruth, Martha, Deborah and Leah (my imaginary mothers) that day was still distant in the future, their losses too overwhelming and real.

"A voice is heard in Ramah, weeping and great mourning. Rachel weeping for her children and refusing to be comforted because they are no more." Matt 2:18

***

GOD DID IT

I've been thinking about Mary and Joseph and the very important part the shepherds played in their life story. It had been a difficult last few months for them. Joseph was likely pitied and Mary certainly shunned. Somehow they survived and most likely looked forward to their son's birth with anticipation and expectation.

Yet when the day arrives, they are strangers in Bethlehem making their home in a stable. They weren't seeking a palace. They were just seeking a bed. I imagine Joseph must have been hurting in his heart, not to be able to provide even that for Mary. I wonder if Mary was experiencing any doubts about God's goodness. Can't you hear the tempter's mocking words, "If this is God's son, surely he would have provided a bed for you in Bethlehem." They had endured nine months of emotional turmoil and then this; this huge disappointment at not finding proper lodging. An artillery of unspoken questions was likely hurtling between them that might have made the silence feel hostile and frightening.

Suddenly it was time. The baby was coming. Joseph did the best he could. Mary did her part. He was beautiful and perfectly formed. And then the shepherds came. Oh, how Mary and Joseph needed to hear the incredible news the shepherds brought via the angelic host that the baby they now held in their arms was the promised Messiah. God did it. He sent the message to them again to erase all doubt.

But what if the shepherds hadn't come? What if they hadn't shared the good news? I don't know the answer to the "what ifs," but what I do know for sure is that it mattered to Mary and Joseph that they did come and that the angels had sent them. Does it not stagger the mind that God entrusted this very needful and important message to a group of shepherds in a field. I have to ask myself why He didn't just send the angels to the stable directly. But then, He is still entrusting His very important and needful message to you and me, isn't He?

The shepherds spread the Word and so must I. I bring you good news of great joy that will be for all the people: A Savior is born to you.

***

JESUS LOST

The headline takes shape in my mind's eye. **SMALL TOWN TWELVE-YEAR-OLD LOST IN HUGE CITY.** It is an understandable tragedy. Every year since His birth, He traveled with His extended family to the city. It was not unusual for Him to ride with relatives along the way, so it was assumed He was with them as they began the journey home. Only at the end of the first day's travel, do they discover He is missing.

His distraught parents immediately retrace their route back to the city and search for him unsuccessfully for three days. His mother's anxiety swells as questions and possibilities (all of them bad) pummel her relentlessly. What does a twelve-year-old do all alone in an unfamiliar city? What does he eat? Where does he sleep? What dangers does he encounter? His father is certain his son is wise enough to take care of himself and avoid needless danger, but for his wife's sake, he knows they must find him.

They finally stumble into the temple to pray and are astonished to discover their son there surrounded by temple officials and calmly involved in a stimulating, energizing and interesting debate. He is seemingly unaware of the anxiety his "lostness" has stirred in his mother's heart.

She speaks. Mary breaks into the debate of these men. Can you hear the anger in her voice? Can you feel the humiliation intended by her words? She attempts to bring Jesus down to size in front of men who moments before marveled at his understanding and ability to answer their questions.

This is Mary accusing God. This is Mary angry at God. This is Mary forgetting God can't be lost. This is Mary forgetting that Jesus is God.

I can relate. I've left Jesus behind and then blamed him for not being there for me. Ah, yes, Jesus is God. Sometimes I forget that, too.

Did you notice the response of Jesus to His mother's accusations? He doesn't remind her that they left him; he didn't leave them. He doesn't play the blame game. Rather, he gently reminds Mary (and me too) that we should know where to find Him. If only we could remember....

***

JUDAS ISCARIOT, THE BETRAYER

I read in Matthew 10, that to Judas, Jesus gave authority to drive out evil spirits and to heal every sickness and disease. The Kingdom of Heaven Is At Hand was the message he was given to preach. He was mandated to heal the sick, raise the dead, cleanse the lepers and drive out demons. He was told to take no money or change of clothing with him and he was to give freely the gifts of healing to those who needed them. He was instructed to be as shrewd as a snake and as innocent as a dove.

Interestingly Judas was warned to be on his guard against men for Jesus said, "they will hand you over to local councils" and "brother will betray brother to death." Did Jesus make eye contact with Judas when He spoke these words?

Jesus went on to say, "Do not be afraid of those who kill the body, but not the soul. Rather fear the One who can destroy both soul and body." "Fear God, Judas," Jesus is saying. I wonder how these words impacted Judas. I wonder how difficult it was for him to be dependent on others for food, shelter and clothing as he traveled. I wonder if he cared too much how others viewed him or feared too much what man could do to him.

I wonder when the seeds of betrayal began to be planted in his heart and what were the choices he made over time that fostered their sprouting and growth.

I wonder what testimony he brought back to the group and who his companion on was this missionary venture documented by Matthew in Matthew 10.

I wonder about the family he grew up in, what his profession was before he joined the disciples, where and how he met Jesus and how he came to be chosen as the group's treasurer. I wonder if he was outgoing or quiet, if he was popular or shunned by most, if he actively participated in ministry, or passively watched from the sidelines.

I wonder if he joined the others to collect the left-over baskets of bread at the feeding of the 5000. Was he one of those trying to cast out a demon from the boy that day Jesus returned from the Mt. of Transfiguration? Was he turning away the children eager to be close to Jesus? Did he join the crowd in calling out to blind Bartimaeus to be quiet? Was he more distraught to see a whole herd of pigs drowning, than he was overjoyed to see a man restored? What was Judas like?

Did he talk over his concerns with Jesus, debate his differing points of view, or ask for understanding of things he couldn't grasp the meaning of? Jesus was present with him day after day for three long years. What did Jesus and Judas talk about?

We have only one incident where Judas is clearly identified prior to that horrible night in the Garden when he betrays Jesus. It takes place, according to John, (John 12) in the home of Lazarus. Judas objects when Mary anoints Jesus with expensive perfume. He questions why the perfume, which was equivalent to a year's wages, wasn't sold and the money given to the poor. It is in this same passage John writes that Judas didn't care about the poor. He was a thief.

Whoa! Imagine it: one of the disciples of Jesus thieving while discipling. Surely Jesus knew it. Yet, there is no indication He did anything about it. As far as we know, Jesus never tried to reform Judas. He never tried to fix the problem of his pilfering.

The relationship between Jesus and Judas fascinates me. I am tempted to cast blame on Jesus for the failures of Judas. Yet, the plight of Judas clearly signals to me that I, and I alone, am accountable for my choices and the behaviors that accompany them. I am responsible for what I believe and what I decide.

Tragically, in Acts 1 Peter refers to Judas as "a guide for those who ARRESTED Jesus." Had he made some different choices, he might have been remembered as a guide for those who ACCEPTED Jesus.

Choices. Epitaphs. Something to think about.

***

PRISON PONDERINGS

Recently I was reading in Matthew 11 where I paused to consider what John the Baptist was thinking in his prison cell. He'd given his life to proclaiming the coming of the Messiah. Now he's wondering if Jesus is really the One. He's realizing that Jesus isn't fulfilling his expectations. He's not acting like a Messiah should act. He's doing the miracles, but discouraging a following. He's not healing a potential army who will join Him in the inevitable conflict when Rome is overthrown. He's healing people and then sending them on their way. John can't make sense of how Jesus is going to bring it all together because he's not doing it the way John would.

John had a lot to think about in prison, a ripe place for the devil to attack. Jesus says, "Don't fall away, John, because I am who I am and not who you think I should be." A fitting reminder to you and me, who, in the prisons of our own making also wonder what kind of God is this Jesus of Nazareth.

***

THE MYSTERY OF HIS WAYS

The actions of Jesus often intrigue me. In Matthew 17:24-27 at issue was the payment of the temple tax. I wonder why Jesus sent Peter fishing for it. That meant that Peter had to collect his gear, go to the water, throw out his line and wait for the fish to bite. The logistics of connecting Peter with the fish that had the coins in its mouth is pretty incredible. Wouldn't it have been simpler and just as miraculous for Jesus to pull the coins out of the air and give them to Peter, saving him from the hassle of fishing? But maybe Peter needed to go fishing and Jesus knew it, so he sent him fishing with a purpose.

When I was in the Philippines, I always tried to find a way for people to do something for me in exchange for money they were requesting/needed. There were times when it would have been way easier just to give them the money they were asking for, but I knew that providing a way for them to earn what they needed always enhanced and strengthened the relationship we shared. Maybe in the same way, Jesus was allowing Peter to have a hand in providing the tax.

I wonder what would have happened if Peter hadn't gone fishing? I wonder how long Peter waited for the first fish to bite. I wonder if there were other unrecorded times when Jesus sent Peter fishing. I wonder if it had something to do with Peter's announcement after the crucifixion and resurrection when he said to the other disciples in John 21:3, "I'm going out to fish."

The actions of Jesus often intrigue me and cause me to wonder. The God who provides does so in a myriad of ways. If I'm not attentive and obedient, I may miss the miracle.

Bekka Siggelkoe

LIFE'S UNFAIRNESS

Matthew 20:1-16 paints for me a picture of life's unfairness. The men hired first agreed to work for a denarius a day. However, as the employer hired new workers all day long, the unspoken expectation of these men is that they would receive less pay. Seems fair and reasonable, wouldn't you say? But they don't. As the pay checks are distributed, it turns out everyone gets a denarius no matter how long they worked.

The workers hired first expected to be paid more. They deserved to get more, didn't they? Wouldn't that have been fair?

What does one do with unfairness and dashed expectations? They are the doorways to temptations to envy, complain and become bitter. Dashed expectations and perceived unfairness can lead to broken relationships, unhappiness and anger. But we all know from experience that life is not fair.

Looking at the passage deeper and longer, I try to put myself into the shoes of the workers who were hired first and I realize that even if I get the same pay as those who came later, I would still prefer to be hired first. Being hired first means I get to be productive; I'm actually doing something; I'm making a contribution. There is the potential for fulfillment and the satisfaction of a job well done. It's an opportunity to learn new skills or perfect ones I know. I don't have to worry about life needs because I'm making a salary.

The guys hired last had to wait most of the day wondering how they would survive without work. The waiting and worrying was perhaps the harder "work."

The reality is God hasn't been fair with me. Instead He's been gracious and generous way beyond what I deserve and I'm so thankful He has.

***

OPPORTUNE TIMES

In Matthew 21: 1-11, the passage begins, "As they approached Jerusalem and came to Bethphage on the Mount of Olives ...." I wonder what Jesus was thinking. The passage continues as He says to two of His disciples, "Go ..." Was He thinking of another "Go" not too far off and spoken to these same men only after He had completed what the Father had given Him to do? Was He thinking ahead to His return in just a few days to this same Mount of Olives not to give instructions, but to "sweat like drops of blood falling to the ground?"

And later as He sat on the donkey, I wonder if this was the more "opportune time" Satan was waiting for? Was this the harder journey than the climb to Golgatha carrying His cross on His shoulders? Did the cheers and shouts of the people at this pinnacle of popularity make Satan's previous offer in the desert more believable and tempting?

Perhaps He looked out over the cheering crowd with compassion? Perhaps He wept in His heart for their lostness? Perhaps He visualized me far in the future and comprehended my need of Him to be my Savior? Perhaps it was during this journey over the cloaks and palm branches that the joy was set before Him, the joy of opening the holy of holies to me and to you? I wonder.

***

THE AUTHORITY OF JESUS

I was thinking of the power and authority of Jesus. In my mind, I joined the crowd of armed hired thugs heading for the Mount of Olives to arrest Jesus. The man next to me keeps smacking his club against the palm of his hand while smacking his lips in anticipation of a fight. He's hoping the guy resists so they can draw a little blood. There's nothing like a fight to get the adrenaline pumping and there's nothing quite like an adrenaline high. I read his thoughts in the lantern light illuminating his eyes which dart here and there in the darkness alert for signs of ambush.

The scene framed forever and etched on my mind is this same man positioned next to Malchus but paralyzed as Peter slices off his friend's ear. In a moment when every man should have fought back, they are motionless.

I see a tableau of men who smell the blood of their comrade and hear his scream of pain piercing the quiet of the night. I take in the sight of men unable to respond in the normal way. Armed, blood-thirsty men eager for a fight are enticed, yet impotent to return the blow. Why?

Because of Jesus. No more of this! That's all He says. And still the men are mute and immobile. Even Malchus, who should have been fighting back, or fleeing while clutching his bleeding head waits and lets Jesus touch him. Such authority stuns me and makes me mute also. I see a rowdy crowd, armed to capture a criminal, captured.

And then the truth that He let Himself be taken by them so He might set me free pierces my heart afresh. I'm awed again by His supreme authority.

***

THE CARPENTER

Mentally I stopped by a carpenter's shop in Nazareth. As I ran my fingers over the top of a table, I mused about what a piece of furniture hand-hewn by Jesus might be worth today. I figured it would fetch a hefty price beyond the scope of my discretionary funds. I surmised that the furniture might be sought after, perhaps even fought over. I suspected it would be treated with honor and respect because of its famous designer and maker.

Jesus wasn't just a carpenter, though. He didn't just make tables and stools. He was the Creator. He hand-fashioned human beings.

Sadly, some humans aren't worth a stool. Sadly, less respect and honor are given to the unborn fetus than might be given to a table made by Him. Sadly, sometimes we love things more than people regardless of what they are, when they were made or by whom.

The Carpenter Creator continues creating.

***

A FRIEND SHARING FAITH

In Mark, chapter 2, I watch while four men approach
Jesus carrying a mat with a man on it. I think to myself
that everyone needs this kind of friend. The man they
were carrying was incapable of getting close to Jesus
on his own, so they brought him. I thought about how
hard it would have been; impossible even, for just one of
those friends, on their own to do what the four of them
together did. I thought of loved ones I know that I keep
praying for and it struck me that maybe I need to rally
some other friends to help me carry this loved one to
Jesus, for there's perhaps no other way to place them at
His feet.

I thought of the four friends. I wondered if they all
knew each other and how it was they were together on
this day. The obstacle they faced when they reached Jesus
required a bigger commitment than just bringing their
friend to Him. I surmise they didn't set out to dig a hole
in a roof, but despite that obstacle, they persevered and
solved the problem together.

Jesus said it was their faith that healed their friend.
That's a sobering thought that my faith might be the
pathway of healing for someone I love, who perhaps has
no faith. I'm thinking about friendship.

I'm thinking about persevering prayer for and commitment to the lost ones I love who've not met Jesus yet. I'm thinking about friends who may want to join me in carrying mats or tearing roofs apart. Whatever it takes.

***

THE TERRIFYING JESUS

The power of Jesus is a fearful thing as the people in the region of the Gerasenes could testify. They had long lived with the demoniac who cut himself with stones, broke his chains and cried out day and night. Mentally ill people frighten me. Working at the state mental hospital during my training as a nurse was fraught with terrifying moments and horror stories of patient antics. But the people of the Gerasenes encountered a terror worse. Jesus.

Jesus, who could question demons: "What is your name?" and command them, "Come out ....." Jesus, who could send a herd of two thousand pigs over a hill and into a lake where they all drowned. Jesus, who could tame a wild man and restore him to his right mind. Jesus. Terrifying Jesus.

This Jesus upsets the way things are, challenges the value of pigs over people, and commands the demons and they obey Him. This Jesus must be sent away. Such was the response of the people in the region of the Gerasenes. You can read the details in Mark 5.

I've always wondered why Jesus would allow the pigs to be destroyed. It bothered me that the pigs were drowned. Today I'm confronted anew with the realization that it bothers me because, in reality, things matter more to me than people. I'm distracted by the pigs and thereby miss the celebration of the person restored. People mattered to Jesus. They mattered more than pigs. So it must be for me if I'm to be like Him.

Psst. Come closer and I'll let you in on a truth I've experienced. Jesus can restore pigs as well as people. Unfortunately the folks from the region of the Gerasenes never got to discover that because they sent Jesus away.

Bekka Siggelkoe

COME APART

In Mark 6:31, Jesus says to his disciples, "Come with me by yourselves to a quiet place and get some rest." Welcome words to work weary wanderers just back from a missionary outreach and continuing ministry to the extent that they didn't even have a chance to eat. Also place into the ministry mix the grief over the death of John the Baptist. So off they went. And then we read "but."

Into every life there is a "but." It signals dashed expectations, disappointment, or failure. In the case of the disciples it seems that Jesus offers what they are longing for only to yank it away from them. Unless there was something deeper the Lord was seeking to teach them. Was He longing for them to be willing to lay aside their personal agendas spontaneously because of love for others like He had? Was He longing for them to see the crowd as He saw them (as sheep without a shepherd) and realize that to fulfill their personal comfort might cost these ones the opportunity to know Him as they did? If He had not offered them rest, they would have sacrificed nothing to feed the multitudes. I've been asking myself this week, "What has it cost me to be a Christian?" When was the last time He offered me the chance to willingly sacrifice for the sake of someone else?

The way we respond to life's "buts" reveals a lot about our character. For the disciples it was a hands-on lesson in denying self. To take up one's cross requires such denial. A hungry multitude placed between the disciples and a solitary place provided the classroom for a life lesson in denial of self. I'm on the lookout today for ways the Lord will provide a similar classroom for me to learn this important life-changing lesson.

***

JESUS LET HIM GO

He was zealously religious. Every law he had stringently obeyed; yet a nagging question pestered him like a buzzing mosquito. Was it enough? Was it enough? Then he met Jesus.

Literally he ran to Him, fell on his knees and blurted out the question he must know the answer to. The text (Mark 10:17-22) says Jesus looked at him and loved him.

Sadly it wasn't love the young man was seeking. He preferred a check list of do's and don'ts that he could master. He wanted outcomes that he could control, as long as it didn't cost him anything. He wanted to know he'd got it right. It was just one thing he lacked, Jesus said. Sadly it was not the answer he expected so he went away, his face fallen.

And Jesus let him go. He let him walk away from love.

***

PARENTING JOHN THE BAPTIST

In Luke 1:67-80, I read the story of a couple who learned that nothing is impossible for God. The writer of Luke introduces me to Zechariah and Elizabeth, for whom the long years of waiting, hoping and praying for a child were now only a painful memory. Long ago they had likely abandoned hope and stopped praying. Their child-bearing years had been discarded involuntarily by the natural process of aging. It was no longer realistically possible for them to conceive and birth a child. Then John was born, a gift of God, a miracle baby.

They knew the child was special and set apart for God, but were they prepared for the desert years ahead? I wonder. Every parent dreams a future for their children. But John, the beautiful miracle baby, would not follow in his father's footsteps and become a priest. Instead he would retreat to the desert hermit like, choosing solitude for a lifestyle while eating locusts and wild honey (a diet any mother might shudder at).

What of Zechariah and Elizabeth during John's desert years? I wonder if they begged him to come home, if they begged him to dress better, eat better, and be less radical and upsetting in his speech. I wonder about the possible heartache of this mother and father. Did they question themselves or God when John left their home for the loneliness of the desert?

The training-up years pass so quickly. Then comes the letting go, when God calls. Did they always know or finally grasp that their beautiful miracle baby boy was not ever really theirs? Such is the ecstasy and agony of parenthood.

I'm pondering possibilities in light of the reality that for God nothing is impossible. I'm realizing, too, that some fulfilled dreams come wrapped in pain.

***

LEPERS AND SHEPHERDS

It just so happened that I encountered two groups of men this week as I read the Scriptures and I found myself wishing that I could have interviewed them, learned what they felt and saw and why they did what they did. I have lots of questions for them both.

The first group had 10 men in it. They were united in their common calamity. They all had leprosy. I find myself wondering why they were all together, how long they had known each other, what experiences they had shared, what they individually believed about Jesus before they met him that day outside a village when they had the bravery to call out to Him to heal them. It seems from the passage in Luke 17 that He merely called back to them that they should show themselves to the priest. I marvel that they set out to do what He said. Why? Why would they do that? I wonder what they discussed along the way. I wonder how they came to be healed. Was it little by little or all at once and all at the same time? Can you even picture or imagine what it must have been like for them? So, then, after they find "on the way" that they are healed, what? How many of them actually continued on to the priest? Only one of them returned to Jesus? Surely they must all have agreed that what they had experienced was a miracle. Surely??? And wouldn't such a miracle naturally result in much praise and thanksgiving? So why is there only one to seek out Jesus? I wonder what became of these men. I wonder if they ever saw Jesus again. I wonder if the lips that failed to thank Him on the day they were healed were lips also raised with the crowds to condemn Him on the day He died. Does it not cause you to be awed at how unconditional is the love of God and how free we are to accept or refuse it?

The other group of men was shepherds. I read about them yesterday. We don't know how many there were tending their sheep in some fields near Bethlehem. We do know that suddenly on this particular night an angel of the Lord lights up the sky. The shepherds don't say anything and the angel makes a proclamation. Not a command. He merely gives them good news of great joy. They could take it or leave it. I wonder if the whole group of men hurried off to see this thing that had happened or if in this group of men there may have been a man who had no desire to see a baby, having already a quiver of his own. I wonder if there was a shepherd who scoffed at the idea that this baby was a Savior. He knew babies have to grow up to be Saviors and he didn't have enough years left in him for such a reality to make a difference to his world. I wonder whatever became of those shepherds. We know where they were at Christmas. I wonder where they were at Easter.

Lepers and Shepherds: men who encountered Jesus. I have a lot of questions for them. They have a lot to teach me.

***

THE ELDEST SON

The story of the prodigal son is found in Luke 15. I can relate to the eldest son whose attributes of good, obedient and hard worker describe me. Jealous, judgmental describe me, too. This time I was struck by the realization that the eldest son's problem was that he didn't grasp the nature of lostness and mercy. The dictionary says that mercy implies compassion that forbears punishing even when justice demands it. Lost is defined as unable to find the way, helpless, ruined or destroyed physically or morally.

The eldest son resented the father's demonstration of mercy, not realizing that he, too, needed and received the father's mercy daily.

It is the father who takes the initiative to seek out the eldest son during the party. It is the father who tries to open the son's eyes to the nature of mercy and lostness as he extends again mercy to his eldest son now lost to the celebration.

I wonder if, after this conversation, the son let himself be found at the party or if he went away to a far distant part of the property to squander his position with the father in anger and unforgiveness. As lost as if he were in a far distant country squandering his wealth in wild living.

A merciful father encounters lostness in both of his sons and extends mercy equally. His is an invitation that demands a response, but first the lostness must be recognized. The youngest son is found. I wonder what ever happened to the eldest.

***

MORE ABOUT THE ELDEST SON

God keeps drawing me back to the story of the elder son in Luke 15. I so identify with him. His statement, "I've been slaving for you" keeps playing over and over in my mind. I'm realizing that he saw himself not as the son with all the privileges and benefits his sonship gave him, but as a slave. He was focused on works and not on relationship.

Being a person who loves parties, I struggle with the elder son's need and desire to have a party thrown for him (or so it would seem from his statement) without having to ask for it. I remember my sister once told me that it always hurt when I came home because of the welcome and hugs Mom would give me. She, who lives near Mom, never gets welcomes and hugs. This elder son's view of the party thing is kind of like that I think. We just want to be tangibly loved in concrete ways. I know that hugs beget hugs. It's just that sometimes it would be encouraging not to have to be the one who always takes the initiative.

But back to the elder son, it would seem that in order for him to get the kind of loving he was longing for, he'd have to become lost like his younger brother when in actuality he'd already been found, but didn't realize it. I guess you could say somewhere along the way he missed the party.

Am I living like a son or like a slave? It's something to think about.

***

A SERVANT GIRL'S STORY

Today I imagined I was a servant girl in Cana at Galilee working with a group of servants to whom Jesus commanded, "Fill the jars with water." (John 2:7) Not difficult. Not unusual. Easily done. A routine task. It felt good to be busy doing something so customary, while the tension surrounding the quickly-depleting wine reserves mounted, permeating the atmosphere. It felt good until He said, "Draw some out now and take it to the master of the banquet."

I've always wondered when the bath water actually became wine. I didn't know it would be wine. I only knew from where I collected it. I knew it was unthinkable to serve the master of the banquet undrinkable water in place of wine.

His command this time was difficult, unusual, and not easily done. This was no routine task. If I and the others escaped with our lives, it would be a miracle. I nevertheless dreaded the outcome. Still a servant obeys whether the task is difficult or easy; usual or unusual; sensible or crazy. A servant obeys.

And the unexpected happens. The bath water is wine. The best wine. And where it came from is a secret I share with Jesus.

Today I imagined I was a servant girl in Cana at Galilee.

***

HE WASHED THE FEET OF JUDAS

Jesus washed the feet of Judas at the Last Supper. It was an act of welcoming hospitality. The one betrayed stooped in vulnerability and love to the betrayer. I wonder which one of the disciple's feet Jesus washed first. I wonder where in the line up Judas was. I wonder if they exchanged words or made eye contact. I wonder how it was that Judas missed being moved by the full extent of Jesus' love poured out on all the disciples that night (according to John 13:1).

I wonder if Judas meant for Jesus to be condemned to death by his betrayal. Perhaps he only wanted to force him to use his power to overthrow the government. Perhaps he reasoned that getting him arrested would incite the kind of conflict he was itching to join.

Poor Judas. He didn't stick around for reconciliation with the risen Christ, for I know that Jesus would have forgiven him. Because of his suicide he never had the opportunity to acknowledge Jesus as the risen Lord and become a foot-washer too.

I suspect it wasn't easy for Jesus to wash the feet of Judas. If he was tempted in every way that we are, and the Bible says he was, I think he may have been tempted to pass on washing Judas' feet. But he didn't.

We are to be like Him.

***

ENDINGS

My friends who know me well, know that when we're watching a movie together that they've seen, I want them to tell me the ending about a quarter of the way into the story. Most don't want to tell me, but if I can know the ending, I can better enjoy the story.

As I was reading the story of the crucifixion (John 19) and imagining the scene of sorrowing people, I found myself wanting to run through the weeping throng shouting, "It's OK. I know how the story ends. All will be well. Don't give up in despair."

As I meditated the scene shifted to friends I have who are hurting and struggling. They also need to know, that there really is a 'happily ever after' and if they know Jesus, He's coming back to take them there. They don't need to give up in despair. All will be well. John 14:1-14 says, "Do not let your heart be troubled. Trust in God, trust also in me (Jesus). In my Father's house are many rooms. If it were not so, I would have told you. I am going there to prepare a place for you . . . and I will come back and take you to be with me."

So there, I couldn't help myself, I just had to tell you the ending.

***

THE MISSING PIECES

Your actions bewilder me, Lord. The scenes are set but so many conversations are missing. Sometimes we get bits and pieces of what was said but rarely the whole. It leaves me pondering many things and asking many questions.

Didn't you long to go to John in prison to comfort and reassure him yourself? I'd love to have been let in on the conversations you had with Lazarus after his resurrection, especially in light of how imminent your own resurrection was.

What off-the-record words did you exchange with the soldiers and guards who escorted you to the cross? Did you share private unrecorded conversations with Judas in an effort to win his heart?

Did any of the servants who had filled the water pots at the Canaan wedding dare to talk with you about what you had done?

Only a few sentences you uttered to a man with leprosy that you healed. The warning you gave him not to tell anyone was not heeded. Did you ever cross paths with him again? Were there more words spoken to a man who dared to disobey his healer?

We get in on some of the questions you were asked along the way, but did anyone ask you to tell them about creating the world? Did anyone question what gave you the most pleasure or what animal, plant, or star especially delights you? Did anyone ask what makes you sad? Who was interested in probing your God heart?

Who were the "others" you saw after your resurrection and what did you say to them? What did they say to you? Did you see Nicodemus or Joseph of Arimethea? What did you say to dismiss the crowd of 5000 you had just fed? Without the help of your disciples how did you manage to leave them and get alone? What was the conversation like when you and Peter climbed in the boat after walking on the water together? Did you talk with the disciples about the cleansing of the temple?

So many conversations lost. So much about your human experience, Lord Jesus, that I long to know.

Diana Stuhr

THE BREAD OF HEAVEN

In John 6:41-59 Jesus said, "I am the bread that came down from heaven." The crowd He was speaking to reasoned He must be a liar because we know Joseph and Mary are the parents of this boy. They could not grasp how He could be both the son of Mary and the Son of God. And because they could not grasp such a possibility, they concluded it must be wrong; He must be wrong.

Such is the logic of unbelief. But the reality of faith is that such impossibility is true. Though we don't know how, we do know that Jesus is both the Son of God and the son of Mary, the Bread who came down from heaven, just like He said.

Such IS the reality of faith.

***

CAMOUFLAGE

Jesus, hungry, spots a leafy fig tree promising juicy fruit. With his taste buds salivating, He spreads the leaves apart only to be disappointed by the barrenness of its branches. There was no fruit. Jesus then curses the tree and causes it to wither and die immediately. The intolerant Jesus doesn't shrug his shoulders and say, "Oh, well, it just must be an off season for the tree." Jesus doesn't give it a second season to produce. Neither does Jesus allow me to be inauthentic. He wants my inside to match my outside. He's not pleased when they don't. Creating camouflage to cover up emptiness doesn't cut it with Jesus. There is no camouflage Jesus doesn't see through.

Camouflaged people shock us, like the mother of a newborn I once knew. On the outside she was a model mother coping just fine. Except that one day her inside and outside collided with tragic results. We mourned the baby's death and our lack of intervention. If only we'd gone beyond the leafy exterior. Jesus longs for us to revel in our freedom to be authentic, to refrain from pretending or covering up. Unless you let me see your emptiness, I can't share with you from my fullness.

Jesus is not a tolerant Savior. He died so we might shed our propensity for camouflage. He died so we might be fully free.

***

PONDERINGS

I've been chewing on the story of Lazarus and his death and resurrection in John 11:1-44. Stimulation for my musings was prompted by a sermon which led me to lay the template of my life over the story of the life of Lazarus and his sisters. Recently a friend of mine died after lingering for more days than I felt were necessary. I wondered what the purpose of her suffering in a semi-comatose state was. The delays of death are a mystery to me, but somehow the God who glorifies Himself in our lives, purposes our life events to bring Him glory, especially those we have no control over. Somehow He glorified Himself as Linda lingered while longing to be home with Him.

Jesus could have come immediately when he learned that Lazarus was sick. He could have healed him, but He didn't. He let him die. The Scripture is clear that Jesus loved Mary and Martha and Lazarus. So you would think that he would come immediately when they called to Him for help, but He doesn't come. I would have thought it would be the very thing that Jesus would do, wouldn't you?

I suspect they didn't feel much loved during the days of His obvious delay. Still He loved them. He knew what the outcome would be, even when they didn't. Trusting His love to be consistent when His love feels so distant is hard. Bottom line: He loved them. Bottom line: He didn't come when they called. Both are true at the same time. That's the mystery of His love.

One of my most precious pictures from this story is that Jesus wept with Mary. He knew that Lazarus would be restored to life (and in a very few minutes) and still He wept with her. He didn't scold her for not trusting Him. He identified with the reality of her pain even though He knew that it would not be a forever pain. I love that about Jesus. I love it that the all-powerful God weeps when His kids hurt. The all-powerful God who can fix anything cries with us when things get broken. I love that about Him.

Ponderables: the delays of Jesus; the silence of God; the lingerings of death.

***

THE TORN CURTAIN

I'm thinking about separation today, about doors and walls and fences and curtains. Being on the outside of closed doors can sometimes be an emotional experience. No one wants to be on the outside wondering if the conversation on the inside is about them, though it rarely is. I hate being on the outside, separated.

That's why the torn curtain into the Holy of Holies touches me so deeply. We can now enter the inner sanctuary. We can go behind the curtain. No more separation. No more mystery. No more insecurity.

Best of all, one day we'll enter the Presence of the Almighty and commune face to face. No more separation of the physical and spiritual. Hebrews 6:19 says, "We have this hope as an anchor for the soul, firm and secure." It's an anchor that holds me fast.

***

TAKE AWAYS

I've been thinking about the soldiers at the crucifixion of Jesus. These men were just doing their jobs. I thought of the soldier who won the day's bonus: the seamless undergarment of Jesus (John 19:22-24) containing the hem the hemorrhaging woman touched. I wonder if he wore the garment boastfully or if he only proudly displayed it like a deer-head trophy. I wonder if he gambled it away again and how many times it may have changed hands before coming to rest, where? Not that the garment had any power or was valuable. Why does the Scripture mention what happened to it?

I thought of the Centurion who stood guard. Perhaps he was a gambler, but did he win or lose the dice toss? Scripture doesn't tell us. All the soldiers at the cross earned their paycheck that day, but the Centurion, after witnessing the death of Jesus confessed, "Surely this must be the Son of God."

Perhaps one soldier took away a piece of cloth, while another took away the fabric of a forever future with the One crucified. With the mouth one confesses and with the heart believes. I've been thinking about the soldiers at the crucifixion.

***

THE DEAFENING SILENCE

There is a silence at the trial of Jesus that is deafening. It is the silence of the defense. Where were the Hosanna Proclaimers and Branch Wavers on that day the crowd cried, "Crucify Him?" Where were the protesters that crucifixion is barbaric? Where were the justice-trackers who cry foul at unfair trials?

Where were those He healed, those He loved, those He forgave; the ones who knew His power was not earthly or temporary? They were silenced, all of them. The quiet at His trial rings loudly in my ears. Only God could orchestrate so one-sided a drama where Jesus stood alone innocent, yet pronounced guilty; a law-giver declared a law-breaker.

Does it not boggle the mind that EVERYONE stood aside while God died?

Diana Stuhr

GOING FISHING AGAIN

Seven men, who are uncertain about their future and mulling over their past, needed a diversion. Peter decided for himself that fishing was what he needed to do; not the fishing for men he'd been called to, but the kind of fishing he'd once done every day. The others joined him. All night they labored, but caught nothing.

How many nights in the past had they faced the morning with nothing to show for their labor? Was Peter thinking of another night, when returning empty-handed, the Master sent them back into the water for the catch of their lives? John must have been thinking of that other night for he's the first to recognize the stranger on the beach who suggests where they should cast their net. Just like the other time. Jesus knows where the fish are. Jesus fills the empty nets miraculously.

It occurs to me that seeing Jesus on this morning meant more to them than full nets. Just to be with Jesus was their heart's desire. They would have gladly left it all again just to be with Him. He was their all in all, their Lord and King.

I'm sobered this morning to realize that some days the fish matter more to me than He does. They are my desire. Some days I battle between choosing the fish or choosing Him. This morning I'm seeing Jesus sitting by a fire on the beach waiting for me to choose. I'm thinking about breakfast with the Morning Star and how tempting it is to pass it up.

***

NOT CHOSEN

When beginning a study of Acts at church, I thought I would read through it to familiarize myself with it in preparation for the study.

I got hung up on chapter 1 verse 23. It's about the apostles finding someone to fill the place that Judas, the Betrayer, vacated. Two men of the group who had been with Jesus from the beginning of His earthly ministry were proposed. Two men whose names were never mentioned until now (at least I don't think they were). It caused me to wonder how many such unnamed people there were who had witnessed the events surrounding Jesus during the three years He traveled and ministered. Don't you wish you could hear all their testimonies?

These two previously unnamed men are thrust into the spotlight as replacements for Judas. I wonder why. Why didn't they instead place everyone's name in a hat and let God pick from the whole group of them? Wouldn't the lot still have fallen to Matthias? Wouldn't it have been less painful for Justus (assuming it was painful for him as it would have been for me)?

I remember letting my name stand for class office my freshmen year in college. I remember the disappointment when I wasn't chosen by the student body. I'm imagining how it might have been for Justus. Not only is he not chosen by God to be an apostle but the whole world for generations after gets to know he "lost" to Matthias.

I wonder what other plans God had for Justus whose heart He knew so well. I wonder if Justus was embarrassed. I wonder how others treated him after his "loss." I wonder if he would have termed it a win/lose situation. I wonder how he responded to the lot falling to Matthias. I wonder what he did with the rest of his life.

What words of encouragement and love did God whisper to Justus in the moment that the lot fell on Matthias? I wonder if he had ears to hear.

As of today, I'm adding Justus' name to the list of people I'm going to look for in heaven. He's someone I've got to meet.

***

PENTECOST

In Acts 2, I read when the day of Pentecost came, they (the disciples) were all together in one place. They were waiting. How many days had they waited? The spirit-filling, spirit-enabling day the Lord had promised was coming, but when was uncertain.

How did they spend their waiting time together? Did they find the time of waiting as hard as I find it? Was there confusion about what they were waiting for? Were they tempted to settle for less than the Comforter Jesus had promised? This Comforter was not someone they had known before. How would they recognize him when he came? How would they know for sure this was it? Did some get discouraged by the waiting? Did they want to give up and move on to something else? Did they doubt they had heard Jesus rightly or understood correctly what He had promised? Who were the encouragers, the ones that reminded them that Jesus was a truth-teller, that what He promised WOULD happen; that they must wait however long it took until it DID happen?

And then out of the blue on one ordinary day it did happen. What were they doing when it suddenly broke in? It came as a sound, not a whisper, but like a violent wind. No corner of the place was unaffected. The Comforter came. The waiting was over. All of them were filled with the promised Spirit, who began immediately to enable them to do a new thing, something they had never before experienced.

I'm thinking that there wasn't a one of them who would say they were sorry they had waited. What do you think?

***

THREE THOUSAND ADDED

Acts 2: 41 says, "Those who accepted his (Peter's) message were baptized and about 3000 were added to their number that day."

Wow, what a harvest. I have to wonder who planted the seed initially and who kept it alive along the way for each one in that crowd? Could we trace some of the 3000 back to the Samaritan woman (see John 4:39) or perhaps to the invalid who went away from the Sheep Gate and told the Jews it was Jesus who had made him well. How many others did he also tell? I wonder.

Maybe it was the family of Zacchaeus (see Luke 19) who shared the good news of their salvation with one of the 3000, or perhaps in one of the many who had come to comfort Mary and Martha in the loss of their brother (John 11:19). The seed of his death and resurrection finally matured and here they were joined with other seekers unaware that their lives were suddenly going to be forever changed.

Each of the 3000 had a personal story, a connection to someone or something that eventually culminated at Jerusalem where they joined a crowd, heard a sermon, and gave their lives to Christ.

I've made it a personal practice over the years as I make friends to ask how they came to Christ and almost always it's because of someone they met or someone they knew. It may not be God's plan for us to be harvesters but He has equipped all of us to be planters.

Thinking of the 3000 inspires me to be better connected, bolder and more prayerful, more aware that unless there's a planting there can't be a harvest. Jesus encourages me to invite as many as I want to the harvest feast He's preparing. So I ask myself, who did I last invite? And who will I invite next?

***

THE CRIPPLE

Verse 16 in Acts 3 says, "By faith in the name of Jesus, this man whom you see and know was made strong . . .." My question is, "Whose faith?"

Perhaps I should back up a bit and tell you that at the temple gate called Beautiful, Peter and John encountered something not so beautiful (or so we would describe it). A forty-year-old cripple who from birth had been carried to this place, lay begging. Forty years. I have to wonder how many times Jesus had passed by him to enter the temple area to preach. I have to wonder if this man had ever listened to Jesus with a longing to be healed. I have to wonder what he knew about Jesus. I have to wonder if he had any faith at all. I have to ask myself if perhaps it was the faith of Peter and John that healed him.

Peter goes on in verse 16, "It is Jesus' name and the faith that comes through him that has given this complete healing to him."

In light of this passage I have to ask myself, "How strong is my faith for the faithless?"

***

GOD ENCOUNTERS

God encounters. I've had them, but none as dramatic as Saul's on the road to Damascus. You can read about it in Acts 9: the bright light, the voice, and the blindness. Seems convincing enough that it was a God thing, but . . . without belief it could have been rationalized away or chalked up to fatigue-induced hallucination. And as for the blindness, it probably would have righted itself in a few days anyway without the Ananias hocus-pocus. Or so someone might think.

I remember praying once with a friend, asking God to restore a lost driver's license. Together we had searched her purse thoroughly. She had already spent two days searching her house and car. The morning after we prayed, my friend phoned to tell me she had found her driver's license lying across her purse "as though someone had placed it there." Those were her exact words, yet when I exclaimed that God or an angel must have visited her house in the night, she responded with, "Oh, we must have overlooked it when we searched my purse." This is a statement of unbelief.

God encounters are recognized by those who believe there is a God; a God who desires to encounter them. No wonder Ananias was afraid. Though God had met Saul, it didn't necessarily follow that Saul had met God. That only happens when one believes.

***

PAUL BREATHING MURDEROUS THREATS

Acts 9.

Saul's passion indicated by the phrase "breathing murderous threats" was to see to it that Christians die. He hated the followers of the way until he met Jesus.

Jesus dramatically got Saul's attention, when Saul armed with letters authorizing him to round up all believers in Damascus for annihilation, was stopped on the way by the crucified Christ. Saul, who saw so clearly the danger of Christians, could suddenly not see at all. He had a direct encounter with the living Christ and it changed him. This man on a murderous rampage enters Damascus holding someone's hand. This leader needed to be led.

It says in the passage that his first three days in Damascus were spent in prayer. Don't you wonder what he prayed? Don't you wonder what the conversations between him and the Christ entailed?

The greater miracle to me in this whole story is Ananias. Talk about a repulsive assignment from God. I love how Ananias tries to change the Lord's mind about what He's asking him to do. As though the Lord didn't already know what Saul had done and what he was planning to do. Can't you hear the earth-shaking thunderous response from God, "Go!" It booms like a thunder clap in my ears and causes me to hit the floor hard every time I imagine it. This is not an "I understand this will be a hard thing for you to do, Ananias, but please do it for me" response from God.

Quivering and fearful though he might be, Ananias does what God asks him to do and THIS IS THE MIRACLE: when he meets Saul, he calls him brother. He touches him and calls him brother, not on the basis of anything Saul has done, but on the basis of what God has said. Ananias believed God and obeyed God. Thank God he did.

I like to imagine the jewels in the crown of Ananias as I read of all the ways God used Saul whose name eventually became Paul; this is the same man who wrote most of the New Testament which continues to draw people to the living Lord.

Today I'm touched by the example of Ananias. I want to be obedient like he was. I want to be so forgiving I can touch my brother and remember he is my brother not on the basis of how he has hurt me but on the basis of what God has done in his life.

***

STEPHEN

There's a picture of Jesus described in Acts 7:56 that I return to now and then. I see Jesus through the eyes of Stephen. The heavens have parted like stage curtains in a theater and Stephen describes what he sees. In the midst of a murderous throng of yelling men intent on killing him, he sees Jesus standing. The sitting Jesus is standing. It is a posture of welcome and eager expectation. Stephen will soon be home and the standing Jesus waits to welcome him. I'm comforted that the same Jesus who sits at the right hand of God the Father also stands. He is alive.

One day the welcoming Jesus will stand with His arms spread wide to envelope me in a big embrace. "You're home," He'll say, as a smile lights up His face.

I love it that the sitting Jesus also stands. It's a compelling picture I return to now and then.

***

BE CAREFUL WHAT YOU PRAY

I bumped into a prayer of Paul's in Romans 1 this week that stopped me abruptly. Paul wrote, "I pray that now at last by God's will the way may be opened for me to come to you." At last – it had been an ardent journey thus far. The route to Rome included Paul's arrest, near flogging, interrogation, mob riots and imprisonment. His second night in prison, it says in Acts 23, "The Lord stood near Paul and said, 'Take courage. As you have testified about me in Jerusalem, so you must also testify in Rome.'" I couldn't help but think of some other words Jesus once said, "Whoever can be trusted with very little can also be trusted with much." Luke 16:10. Being faithful in Jerusalem was an important prerequisite for ministry in Rome.

But the journey to Rome was fraught with problems. Even after the Lord's personal visit, there was the shipwreck on Malta. (Acts 27) It was another delay, another difficulty, another reason to mope and despair, but not for Paul. For Paul, Malta was a place of ministry, of making friends, of sharing Christ (Acts 28) Would it be days, weeks, months, years? Paul didn't know.

He remained faithful, however, day by day in the little things, in the Malta spots where snakes bite and life is hard. Such is the journey of faith. Thus do dreams come true. Paul eventually arrives in Rome.

How about you? Are you vitally involved where you are, or stagnantly dreaming of where you long to be?

***

SHARED DROPLETS

In Romans 11 Paul writes about his longing that he and the fellow believers in Rome be mutually encouraged by each other's faith. It got me to thinking...

It was only a drop of faith I brought to our coffee chat, my friend, but in the miracle of multiplication, the drop you also brought became mixed with mine as we talked of spiritual things. When we parted, I realized our drops had become a spring of gushing water invigorating our individual faiths. I love this mixing of our meager faiths which when blended becomes mighty faith. The mutual encouragement experienced as we talked pleased the Father from whom the drop of faith we brought each other was given. We know He can set aflame such droplets (as He did for Elijah in I Kings 18) while at the same time quench our thirsty souls. It happened again today when I offered my drop and you offered yours. I left you less thirsty and set aflame for Him. Thank you for the drop you brought. Today it became an ocean in my soul and encouraged me to press on.

CONFLICT IN THE CHURCH

I was reading in Philippians 4 about Euodia and Syntyche, friends of Clement and Paul, fellow workers. Both were suffering for Jesus while fighting with each other. Over what, I wonder? I wonder who started the conflict and why. Was it a difference of opinion spurred by the need to be right? Perhaps. Was it a theological issue spurred by conviction? Maybe. Was it a difference of popularity spurred by envy? Could be. Was it a difference of position spurred by the need for recognition? Not out of the realm of possibility.
Paul pleads that they would agree. Agree about what?
Agree to stop fighting and start loving?
Agree to follow Christ's example?
Agree to make Christ their focus and not each other?
Agree that the first shall be last?

I wonder whatever happened to Euodia and Syntyche. Did the wounded keep on wounding? Was Clement or someone else able to mediate reconciliation? To all the Euodias and Syntyches, I plead like Paul: stop fighting each other and start fighting the enemy for the heart of lost ones who have yet to realize the battle's been won by the Savior.

***

Mackenzie Phillips

MY HEART HIS TABLET

I've been thinking about who is written on my heart. Paul said to the Corinthians in II Corinthians 3:3 & 4, "You are our letter, written on our hearts, known and read by everybody. You show that you are a letter from Christ, the result of our ministry, written not with ink but with the Spirit of the living God, not on tablets of stone but on tablets of human hearts."

This month He wrote you on my heart: You who came with tears of disappointment because of the rejection of a loved one, You who said yes when you should have said no, You who feared the surgery would not go well, You who doubted that Jehovah-Jirah would provide, You who felt the sting of jealousy, You whose anger formed the words your tongue spit out, You who grieved a loved one gone.

He wrote you on my heart. I recited your name to Him in prayer.

***

SHELTERED UNDER HIS WING

I've been reflecting lately on Colossians 1:15-21, but especially I've been chewing on verse 17: "He is before all things and in Him all things hold together."

I've been thinking about what a different world we might live in, if just for a moment God let go; if just for a moment He stopped holding all things together.

For example, I learned recently that a single (not as in unmarried) lobster lady lays thousands of lobster eggs at one time. What if every lobster egg became a fully grown lobster?

Or what if, all of a sudden, all the color left the world and everything became black and white?

Or what if, for an instant, we all stopped aging. What if our world was made up entirely of thirteen-year-olds?

Or what if the sun stepped out of orbit and moved towards the earth or further away?

The list of "what-ifs" is endless. I'm thankful today that God holds all things together every day all day long. I'm also thankful that this same God has a hold of me.

***

GANGRENOUS TEACHING

Hymenaeus and Philetus, were workmen who wandered away. They are described as successful teachers; successful because their teaching spread like gangrene. Only it wasn't the truth they were teaching. They were destroying the faith of some, not deepening it.

Who did these men listen to? What godless chatter did they indulge in? What conversations led them to becoming not like Christ? Talking away they failed to notice the pathway under their feet was no longer narrow.

The Lord knows who are His. We can identify them, too. They speak to one another in psalms, hymns and spiritual songs. They admonish one another with all wisdom. Their speech is seasoned as with salt.

Paul warned the Ephesians to let no unwholesome talk escape their tongue. Trained tongues have masters who listen well and talk little.

Teaching pondered again today by a recovering chatterbox who doesn't want to follow in the footsteps of Hymenaeus and Philetus. (See II Timothy 2: 17)

***

TRANSFORMATIONS

God is in the business of turning people around. He picks the most unlikely-to-succeed types for some of His biggest assignments. Saul would not have been my pick for "chosen instrument to carry my name" candidate. Yet God knew what He had in mind for Saul/Paul to do. You might say he was hand-picked by God. I wonder if you'd raise your hand and beg, "Please, God, pick me" when you consider the following "assignments" God gave Paul:
3 days of blindness with no guarantee it wouldn't be
    forever
5 different lashings 41 times each
3 times beaten with rods
1 time stoned
3 times shipwrecked
1 day and night in the open sea
having to be constantly on the move
danger from rivers, from bandits, from Gentiles, from
    false brothers
having to go without sleep, without food and water
being cold and naked experiencing the daily pressure of
    concern for all the churches
imprisonment

Such is the life of one hand-picked by God to do great things for God. It's not a cushy job, but there are rewards. "Now there is in store for me," says Paul, "the crown of righteousness, which the righteous Judge will award to me ..." II Timothy 4:8

Dare I ask, "Please, God, choose me?"

PEEKS INTO HEAVEN

I was reading Revelation 4:1-11. It struck me that you have to look to see open doors. I wonder how many peeks into heaven; I've passed up because I failed to look. Perhaps that is what Jesus meant when he talked of those who have eyes to see.

The scene John paints in this passage seems so Hollywoodish to me. The sights and sounds are animation-like, a razzle dazzle, if you please. It is not the hushed holy somber-like scene in the throne room that I sometimes envision. Still it is the reverence for the Holy that grips me as I stand near John in my imagination, taking it all in.

It is the attraction of God Almighty that draws my gaze from the glittering golden crowns and my love for Him swells as the music crescendos with "You are worthy."

Indeed, may the Worthy One tune your heart and train your eyes whenever you approach the manger, so that if He grants it, you won't miss the peek into Glory that leaves you face down with the elders acknowledging He is indeed worthy to receive glory, honor, and power.

***

135

THE TOURIST OR THE PILGRIM?

The journey through life is traveled differently by the tourist and the pilgrim. The tourist, camera in hand, captures images of life making them still; caught in a moment of time to be remembered that way.

The pilgrim sits quietly and soaks up movement, receiving life in all its dimensions; the choreography not lost in grainy captured shots, but vibrant in its changing postures. The impatient tourist hurries to the next shot at life. The serene pilgrim soaks up the thirst-quenching beauty of each moment offered, discovering the hidden things revealed in the stillness of one who waits expectantly.

The encumbered tourist, with camera case and well shod feet becomes weary in the wanderings and longs for what is still ahead though uncertain it will satisfy. The pilgrim, empty handed and barefoot, plods slowly through landscapes ready always for holy ground happenings that require one to be shoeless. This one finds satisfaction in each savored moment and the untarnished treasures that he carries in his heart not in his hands.

Some days I'm a tourist rushing here and there. But thank God for the carved out days in the calendar when I leave camera and shoes behind and the pilgrim in me sets off on the highways of my heart where I find myself and the One who is my travel guide in terrain unfamiliar

to me but not to Him. On pilgrim days I recognize Him
more quickly.

Jesus walks with me
On tourist and on pilgrim days.
The Bible tells me so.
But especially on tourist days
I travel Emmaus Road by-ways
And He's the Stranger I don't know.
I have no idea it is Him.
Life's harshness clouds all I see,
So hidden is the Savior
Who said He'd walk with me.
On pilgrim days
I pause and wait and often find
The cloudiness is lifted
And I'm no longer blind.
I see the One who walks with me
Is adequate for all I face,
So with courage I press on
Allowing Him to set the pace.
Jesus walks with me
On tourist and on pilgrim days.
This I truly know.
I prefer the pilgrim days
As pressing on we go.

***

HEM AND HEART

I love the story of the hemorrhaging woman who
traversed a crowd of people to get close enough to Jesus
to touch the hem of His garment. He was her last hope
for healing and it worked. The minute she caught hold of
His hem, she was healed. But was it enough? My sister,
Donna, hit the nail on the head when she mentioned that
there was more than one kind of healing. Jesus stopped to
identify the woman because there was the matter of her
heart. It needed healing too.
She touched His hem
He touched her heart.
She came to Him,
His work of art.
The bleeding stopped.
Healed
She went her way
She touched His hem
He touched her heart
One fateful day.

***

DARE TO BE A PHOEBE

I read in Romans 16 about Phoebe, the helper commended by Paul. She was a servant of the church and worthy of sainthood according to Paul.

Can't you just picture it? Everybody loves Phoebe. She is always doing something helpful for someone else. Where does she get all that energy, people wonder. The jealous types hope she's on drugs. Any flaw in her squeaky clean profile is a feather in their cap. Oh, they wouldn't wish her to a lion's den. That would be too severe, but a plunge off the pedestal others put her on wouldn't hurt her or them.

Phoebe, a helper, servant of the church, saint. Hated, I suspect by the jealous types.

Dare to be a Phoebe,
Dare to serve as Christ would
Dare to love your neighbor
Dare to be all good.

Dare to be a Phoebe
Meeting someone's need
Dare to listen to the Savior
Dare His Word to heed.

Dare to be a Phoebe
No matter what the jealous say

Dare to man the trenches
Dare to give your heart away.

Bekka Siggelkoe

NO GLUE NEEDED THERE

I received a cartoon in the mail recently. It pictures Dennis the Menace sticking his head out of a room at the top of the stairs calling down to his parents, "I'm gonna need some love and understanding and a whole (my word) lot of glue up here."

I couldn't help chuckling as I pictured myself popping my head out of the portals of heaven and calling down to anyone who's listening, "I've found perfect love, complete understanding and not a single thing broken up here."

Think about it with me. In heaven no wrongs need to be righted, no slights need to be confronted, no wounded hearts need to be mended, no enemies need to be defeated and no wars need to be fought. Jealousy, fear, bitterness and hatred have all been dealt a final blow. We won't ever battle them again.

Rung-by-rung I'm climbing the stair steps to heaven with a new song in my mouth. It goes like this:

There's no need for a whole lot of glue up in heaven
There's no need for glue over there.
Nothing's cracked
Nothing's broken
All the fixin' is through
There's no need for a whole lot of glue.

There's no need for more lovin'
For lovin' flows free
There's no need for forgiveness
For perfect we'll be.

There's no need for a whole lot of glue up in heaven
There's no need for glue over there
Nothing's cracked
Nothing's broken
All the fixin' is through
There's no need for a whole lot of glue.

Now is that not good news!!! I can't wait to pop out of a
portal. How about you?

***

HOW WILL I SPEND MYSELF?

I was reading in Joshua 1 this week and camped on God's words to Joshua, "Do not be terrified." I camped there because I was confessing to a friend earlier that I get terrified easily. I realized as I pondered God's command in this passage that I'd rather not expend my energies in battling fear.

Instead I want to spend myself in:
Fixing my eyes on the Author and Perfecter of my faith.
Setting my mind on things above.
Running the race with perseverance.
Putting on the armor of God daily.
Clothing myself with love.
Seeking first His kingdom.
Shunning evil.
Clinging to what is good.
Hallowing His name.
Letting my light shine.
Offering myself as a living sacrifice.
Bearing the burdens of others.
Forgiving as I've been forgiven.

Ah, yes, I'd rather not waste my energies being terrified. He who said, "Do not be terrified," also said, "I am with you always." I think if I really connected with that reality, nothing could make me afraid. I think if I really connected with that reality, I would be very brave.

***

JUST SHOW UP

Recently I read a verse I hadn't really seen before. It's found in Matthew 28:17. It says, "When they saw Him they worshipped Him, but some doubted."

Remember the old saying, "seeing is believing?" Perhaps that's not always the case. The eleven disciples showed up where they were supposed to be and found the previously dead and buried Jesus there too. The resurrected Lord was in their midst. Still some doubted. I wonder what they doubted, don't you?

I've heard people say that if they could have seen Jesus after His resurrection, then they would believe in Him. Maybe; but maybe not. I've heard people say that the disciples who saw Jesus had advantages over us because they were able to see Him. Apparently not.

Among the eleven disciples gathered after the resurrection, there were worshippers and doubters. Is that not amazing? And all of them received the same instructions from Jesus, "Go ye." Is that not amazing, encouraging, affirming and exciting?

> I wonder if from the seeds of doubt
> God can grow a faith tree, sturdy, strong and true.
> Perhaps just showing up
> And watching out for what He'll do
> Is what it's mostly all about?
> Just showing up, despite your doubt.

***

THE ANGELS MISSED HIM

The angels missed him
While Mary rocked the babe to sleep
And wise men hunted
Where shepherds tended sheep.
Mystery enveloped the celestial city.
Angels questioned the discarded royal robe,
As they watched the happenings on a distant globe.
Why had He left them
To clothe Himself in human flesh
And lie helpless on the straw
Within the manger crèche?
The angels longed to know.

***

IT'S A WONDERFUL THING

It's a wonderful thing
To be loved by the King.
It's a wonderful thing
To be loved.

There's a song I can sing
About the love of the King.
It's a wonderful thing
To be loved.

His whispers descend
On His promise I'll depend.
He's a King who sends us His love.
He calls us His friend
He's near 'till the end.
I can sing of the King and His love.

It's a wonderful thing
To be loved by the King.
It's a wonderful thing
To be loved.

***

CUDDLING WITH GOD

Cuddling with God in the morning
Climbing up into His lap
Playing and giggling with Jesus
Talking about this and that.

He tells me how much He loves me.
He puts the words in a song.
I feel His arms tighten round me.
Certain that here I belong.

These morning moments together
Give me courage all through the day.
I couldn't leave home uncertain.
He's at my side all the way.

***

GOOD WORKS

Good works
He's prepared good works
Good works for me to do.
Good works
He's prepared good works
Good works for me and you.

Before I was formed
He dreamed good works for me
Attaching bones to make my frame
He knew what I would be.

Good works
He's prepared good works
Good works for me to do.
Good works
He's prepared good works
Good works for me and you.

He smoothed my flesh
And carved my face
Thinking all the while
Of all the ways I'd share His grace.
Look, can you see Him smile.

Good works
He's prepared good works
Good works for me to do.
Good works

He's prepared good works
Good works for me and you.

When He placed me in the womb
He had in mind good works I'd do
Good works from birth to tomb
Good works for me and you.

Good works
He's prepared good works
Good works for me to do.
Good works
He's prepared good works
Good works for me and you.

***

DEMONSTRATED LOVE

Demonstrated love
In a ram caught in a bush
In a bush bursting with flame
In a parted sea
In a God who knows my name.

Demonstrated love
In a lion's den
In a prison cell
In a fiery furnace
And beside a well.

Demonstrated love
For a widow's grief outpoured
For a demoniac restored
For a daughter no longer dead
For a multitude without bread.

Demonstrated love
For the leper (one of ten)
For a lame man brought by friends
For a blind man calling out
For a seeker filled with doubt.

***

LIVING STONES
Based on I Peter 2:4-11

Living stones
Building blocks
The corner stone
HIM.

Chosen and precious
The foundation
The bedrock of our faith
HIM.

Some men stumble
Some men fall
Those who trust build
And become
A chosen people
A royal priesthood
A holy nation
A people of God
Praising
HIM.

***

WORDS

Being made in His image,
Daily we create.
With words we make
Things that weren't come to be
Brick by word brick
The syllables are mortared tight
To make a wall of unscaleable height
Creating silence, barring light.
Plank by word plank
Nouns and verbs are nailed in place
To make a bridge
Where back and forth we race
Connected.

Words. Rippling off the tongue.
Joyfully is each sentence strung
To make one laugh with glee
Or produce an atmosphere of fun
Where all who watch it want to be.

Words. Powerful in their intent
Are like arrows sent.
They make one hurt, make one cry
Sometimes make one wish they could die.
Arrows to the heart
Are these words that sting and smart.

With words we create
Things that weren't before

Daily we build or destroy
With just a word
Made in His image
Thus we are
To beautify or scar.

***

SONGLESS

I met a man once
Who spent songless days
Stringing and unstringing his instrument of praise.
No music flowed.
No sound was heard.
But
Busy, busy and without a word
The man worked on stringing and unstringing
Until his singing days were gone.
And so I think
The God of Song
Maker of Music
Waits for me.
Will I spend my days in ceaseless praise
Or will I songless be?

***

THE TALLEST TREE

There was once a tree
Who lamented every day.
He longed to be the tallest tree.
For this he would always pray.

As years passed by
On the hillside he grew.
Stretching tall and wishing hard
Was all that he could do.

He could never top the first tree
Looming high over his head.
His faith in God diminished
It seemed his dream was dead.

How sad-the tree was blind
To the hillside where he stood.
He had always been the tallest tree,
The tallest in the wood.

***

IMMEDIATELY

In Matthew 4 we read that Jesus is walking beside the
    Sea of Galilee and he sees two brothers and calls
    to them. Two fishermen responded. They left
    immediately,
their nets,
livelihood,
homes,
friends.
They didn't ask, "What's in it for me?"
They didn't ask if the trade-off would be fair in the
    leaving.

They left immediately.
They didn't
ponder,
procrastinate,
grieve,
cleave,
consider.

They left immediately.
They didn't
clean up their nets,
tidy up their affairs,
have good-bye parties,
pack a bag.

They left immediately.
Both of them.

They were two brothers on an adventure
leaving the known for the unknown,
the certain for the uncertain,
sameness for newness,
the predictable for the unpredictable.

They hadn't fished for men before. They didn't know how
        to fish for men.
They didn't know
how hard it would be,
what results they could expect,
what men they would "catch."
They just left immediately.

James and John followed suit.
They, too, left immediately.
They left their boat and their father;
a needful possession and a valued relationship.

Others might say they were impulsive,
foolish,
uncaring,
thoughtless,
selfish,
to leave so immediately.

I wonder why they did. What was it about Jesus that
        compelled them to leave?
Immediately?

***

CLAY JARS
From II Corinthians 4:7

Clay jar treasure chests; that's what we are
God's hidden His glory in this clay jar.
There'll be no confusion,
There'll be no mistake,
There'll be no denying,
No heated debate.
God's power all surpassing, sufficiently great
Is recognized rightly in our humble estate.
Clay jars, clay jars
His treasures He's placed in clay jars.

Bekka Siggelkoe

CHILDHOOD MIRRORS

Childhood mirrors
Held by other's hands
Give us an image of ourselves
A persona behind which we stand.
Though it may be distorted
And not resemble us a bit,
We see the image clearly
And forever try to fit who we really are
Into the image others see
Failing to free our true selves
To become all that we could be.
And then we wonder why
We are never satisfied
When we fail to discover who we really are
Deep inside.
When our authentic being is forever shelved or denied.
We will always believe the mirrors that others hold
And live an unreality until we're old.

***

WE'RE CROSSING OVER

We're crossing over, God and I
Crossing over by and by,
Crossing over the Jordon River.

Going to take the land by surprise
Crossing over at sunrise.
We're crossing over, God and I
Crossing over by and by
Crossing over the Jordon River.

Killing giants as we go
Milk and honey overflow.
We're crossing over, God and I
Crossing over by and by
Crossing over the Jordon River.

The Promised Land is finally mine
It's my Father's grand design
We're crossing over, God and I
Crossing over by and by
Crossing over the Jordon River.

***

JUDAS

Judas, one of the chosen few.
There were only 12 of them
Handpicked by Jesus
12 faithful law-abiding men.

For 3 ½ years always at His side
Watching as He healed
Jesus, Lord, Master, Savior, Guide
Jesus, the Crucified.

When did you decide to turn away?
To betray?

Did you find the cleansing of the temple unsettling,
Disturbing, unwise?
Was that when Satan closed your eyes
To the Divine Son?

Were you jealous when Jesus took Peter, James and John?
Was that the start?
Was it then the seed of betrayal
Was planted in your heart?

When did you decide to turn away?
To betray?

Did you ever love the Savior
Or was it all a sham?

Were you longing for Messiah?
Did you seek the Great I Am?

When did you decide to turn away?
To betray?

Was it on the storm-tossed sea
Your fear made a pathway wide
For the father of lies
To enter your heart and hide?

When did you decide to turn away?
To betray?

Was the soil of your heart already hard
When the parable of the seeds was first told?
Did the miracle of feeding the multitudes
Allow Satan his best foothold?

When did you decide to turn away?
To betray?

Were you not amazed by His power
To raise a widow's son?
Were you not aware of all the battles
With the enemy He had won?

All the roads you traveled with Him
Walking by His side
All the miracles you witnessed
All the tears He cried.

When did you decide to turn away?
To betray?

When the demoniac was healed
And all the demons fled
Were you delighted at the healing
Or mourning for the pigs now dead?

When did you decide to turn away?
To betray?

There was a bent-over woman
He made straight and tall.
But He healed her on the Sabbath.
Were you agreeing that wouldn't do at all?

Were you always critical in your heart?
Were the seeds of betrayal there from the start?
Did your choices make them sprout?
Were you always filled with doubt?

He washed your feet.
He offered you bread.
You rushed to the street.
To cutthroats you fled.

When did you decide to turn away? To betray?
Judas did you ever love Him who gave His life for you?

***

FORGIVENESS

Forgiveness seekers
Are forgiven by the One who died
Yet held in contempt
By the colleague at their side;
Forgiveness seekers cling
To the crucified
And leave the harvest broken
Rejected and denied
The very forgiveness
For which the Savior died.
It is forgiveness withheld by a colleague
Clinging to his pride
No wonder that at Gethsemane
Our Savior cried.

***

IN HIS HAND NO STONE

She is a sinner, condemned, but by whom?
Can you Pharisees, unclean yourselves, demand her
      doom?
With righteous fury and urgent hurry, you thrust her at
      His feet.
Law Giver and Lawbreaker now have a chance to meet.

She knows she's guilty.
She thinks she's bad,
But this is the worst nightmare
She's ever had.

Betrayed by a lover.
Dressed by her foes.
Carried like garbage,
In her torn, soiled clothes.

You drop her in the midst of a crowd.
You list all her sins, in voices out loud.
Then stooping to gather a stone in each hand,
You call to the Teacher, you shout a command.

"Now what do you say?" You shout.
Your plan is well set.
You were sure that you had Him.
And yet . . .

You watch as He stoops.
You look as He writes
You cluster in groups
You're ready to fight.

You question again.
You're not giving in
And suddenly He stands,
His face looking grim.

"The first stone must be thrown
By the one without sin."
Your shocked faces reflect the power of His word.
He, who is Law Giver, Earth Maker, Redeemer and Lord.

One by one you drop your stones to the ground.
You each turn away, no one making a sound.
Adulterer and Savior are left all alone.
In His sinless hands...
There isn't a stone.

DO YOU WANT TO BE HEALED?

A pallet
A sickness
A pool
A question.

A way of life
For one grown used to the pallet
And the pool.
Healing would mean change.
Leaving the familiar, safe place of pool and pallet.
Healing would mean work, responsibilities, obedience.
But to stay, would it not be foolish?
When Christ says, "Take up your mat and walk,"

Who wouldn't go?
Who wouldn't
With mat in hand
Walk away from the pool
At His command?

Wouldn't you?
I would.

***

Bekka Siggelkoe

SPEAK, MAN!

You come to me with doubts and accusations?
You would accuse God?
Let me question; answer me this.
When the earth's foundations were set in place,
Where were you?
When the morning stars a chorus made
As angels shouted gleefully and the cornerstone was laid
Where were you?
Were you helping me?

Did you help to set the boundaries of the sea?
Or shut the doors and bars to keep it in its place?
Did you weave the clouds or form the darkness vast and
     deep?
Where were you?
Were you not asleep?

Have you traversed the vastness of the earth?
Or called the morning star at break of day
To give you light upon your way?
Did you mold the earth making features three-
     dimensional?
Tell me if you know?
Lead me to my storehouse full of snow.
Show me the place from where the lightening springs.
Point me to the spot from where the East wind sings.

And what of the storm, the rain?
Who fathers them? Please explain.

What of the wild animals or the stars?
Can you tame them, hold them, name them?
Are they yours?

You, man, would accuse God,
The CREATOR GOD?
You, whom I made of sod.
You would accuse me,
CREATER GOD?

Speak, man. Speak. If you can.

***

BECAUSE HE HAS GIVEN

Ribbon-wrapped moments
One piled on the other.
Ribbon-wrapped moments
A chance to discover,
He is the ribbon
His life for mine.
Because He has given
These moments I'm livin'
They're eternal in time.

Joy-splashed mornings
One piled on the other.
Joy-splashed mornings
A chance to discover.
He is the joy source
His life for mine.
Because He has given
These moments I'm livin'
They're eternal in time.

Merciful new days
One piled on the other.
Merciful new days
A chance to discover.
He is the Grace Gift
His life for mine.
Because He has given
These moments I'm livin'
They're eternal in time.

Eternal musings
One piled on the other.
Eternal musings
A chance to discover.
He is Forever
His life for mine.
Because He has given
These musings I'm livin'
They're eternal in time.

***

SEND ME A SONG

My harp in the trees
I'm down on my knees
I'm begging you, please
Lord send me a song.
A song I can sing
In this foreign land
A song of the things
That for me you have planned
Lord, send me a song.

The Babylonians tease
Their tauntings don't cease.
I'm begging you, please
Lord send me a song.
A song I can sing
In this foreign land
A song of the things
That for me you have planned
Lord, send me a song.

Chains and decrees
My realities these.
I'm begging you, please
Lord send me a song.
A song I can sing
In this foreign land
A song of the things

That for me you have planned
Lord, send me a song.

A song of release,
Of blessings with peace.
I'm begging you, please
Lord send me a song.
A song I can sing
In this foreign land
A song of the things
That for me you have planned
Lord, send me a song.

***

A BRAND NEW DAY

The whole day stretches before me
A parchment white
Without scratches or markings
Without color or light
I've minutes to spend from morning to night.
As I crawl into bed at the end of this day
What will the parchment contain and display?
What were my thoughts?
What did I pray?
What work did I do?
What words did I say?
The etchings are permanent
Each marking, each stain.
I can't redo my history
Nor relive a single frame.
Jesus sees it all
As the parchment patterns form
How I've lived my moments
Whether in the sunshine or the storm.
At day's end would I hang this parchment
Unafraid for all to see?
Would observers say my God was glorified?
Would they say that Jesus lives in me?
The parchment white
Unmarked
Unstained
Uncolored

Bare
A new day lies before me
A cache of minutes waiting
To be spent with utmost care.

***

THIRSTY

Thirsty, Lord, I'm thirsty
Parched by the desert heat
I bow surrendered, yielded,
Staring at Your feet.

Giver of water, Living water
Pure and freshly drawn
Pour over me
Until my thirst is gone.

Thirsty, Lord, I'm thirsty
The desert stretches vast and long
I bow and beg for water
Pure and freshly drawn.

***

MY DAD

My Dad, He planted his seed and went on his way
Not knowing his resemblance would follow one day.
The seed he had planted would in nine months become
A child full of laughter, good looking and fun
Who with longing would wonder what he was like.
This one who had planted in passion one night.
Was he fearful or brave?
Was he handsome or tall?
What did he dream? What did he crave?
Was he creative at all?
Was he mostly happy or mostly sad?
Was he always good or consistently bad?
Unfortunately, He'll never know the daughter he had
And she'll never hug him and call him her Dad.

***

PRAISING HIM
Based on Psalms 66

I'll raise my voice with shouts of joy
I'll clap and sing and dance and laugh
I'll tell of all your awesome deeds
Done on my behalf.
So great is Your power
Sovereign Ruler of all
I'm humbled to fathom
You wait for my call.
My voice you know well
Your love I embrace
It took you to hell
My sins to erase.
Hear my shouts of joy
Watch me clap and sing and dance and laugh
As I recall your awesome deeds
Done on my behalf.
Thank you, God
Lord and King
Thank you, God
My praises ring.
Thank you God
My song I bring
To thank you, God,
For everything.

While being thankful, suddenly:

The faces of friends
Parade through my mind
Treasures of heaven
Gathered with time
Pleasures are passing
Worldly gain is soon gone
Lasting forever
Are friendships made strong.
Centered in Jesus
Forgiven all wrong
We're companions together
The whole journey long
Treasures of heaven
Gathered with time
The faces of friends
Parade through my mind.

***

HIS SEAMLESS GARMENT

His seamless garment is thrust aside
By men with roughened hands
Who nail Him to a cross
At the Pharisees commands.

His seamless garment lies in the dust
Until their work is done
With each cross positioned on a hill
They'd finally have some fun.

His seamless garment becomes
The object of their game
"It should be won, not torn apart,"
One of them exclaims.

His seamless garment was but a rag
If only they had known
His death would win for them
A royal robe and throne.

He let go the seamless garment
And counted it not loss
He let go the seamless garment
And chose instead the cross.

***

SHE IS LOVED
Based on portions of Psalms 5

Expectantly waiting.
She is stilled after much speaking
To a God
Who responds
Who protects
Who blesses.
In the stillness,
In the waiting,
First one note and then another
Skips around the perimeter of the silence
Finally penetrating it.
A song is birthed.
Joy bubbles forth.
The one who waits is glad.
In the cocooned safety of the Father's arms
Protected
The one who waits
Sees
The shield of blessing
And believes, finally
She is loved.

***

HIS MAGNUM OPUS SONG

A work in progress
You and me
A shaping work
Uncomfortable though it be
And in between the striking blows
The shaping needs, we bleed
And crave to know
Where we belong.
Not ready yet for the artist's gallery
We wait,
A motley throng.
The beauty is becoming
Our artist God is never wrong.
We are a masterpiece in the making.
We are His magnum opus song.

***

GOD COMES NEAR
Based on Matthew 21:16b.

Out of the mouths of babes
And nursing infants
You have perfected praise
Love songs in an instant.

Giver of Praise Songs
Grave Conqueror mighty and strong
Gracious Redeemer, Lord God my King
Glorious Deliverer, let the hallelujahs ring.

Trampled and broken
With no song on her lips
She hears mercy words spoken
As the wine of His love she now sips.

Blinded in darkness he sits.
Various noises tickle his ear
They give his life meaning only in bits
Until the Savior draws near.
A leper, unclean
Hides in a crowd unseen
Except the One, aware
That he's there;
A Savior who touches
What others declare,
Unclean.

Crippled he lies, lost and aloof
Until carried by friends, lowered down through a roof
He's healed at the feet of the Bearer of Truth.
Thankful for friends and a roof torn apart
He gets a glimpse of the Savior's merciful heart.

So many stories of people He touched
So many love songs by those He loved much
Savior we come like the ones long ago
Crying for mercy, for the love songs you sow.
Longing for relationship, it's You we want to know.
Send us the seeds from which loves songs will grow.

***

TRIBUTE TO A MOM

Mother of others
And mother of me
Though not knit in your womb
It's still plain to see
Your loving touch has fashioned me.

You listened
You loved
Wise counsel you gave
How sorely I miss you
How unwelcome your grave.

I want to remember
And keep you close to my heart
For you helped me to grow.
You were a treasure to know
From the start.

Your gentleness
Your smile
Your flowers in bloom
Your patience
Your kindness
The way you lit up a room.

The meals at your table
The prayers on the way.
Memories we made
All through the day.

Unwelcome your death
Unwelcome your grave
Unwelcome your absence
Your presence I crave.

Mother of others
And mother of me.
I love you, I thank you
I miss you terribly.

***

SABBATH

Momentary connection with the Divine
Immersed in His splendor we find
Hope
Momentary connection with the reigning King
Immersed in His glory we sing
Joy
Momentary connection with He who provides
Immersed in His generosity we confide
Faith
Momentary connection with the One ever present
Immersed in His nearness we lament
Sin
Momentary connection with the One resurrected
Immersed in His living we accepted
Love.
Momentary, yet daily
Fleeting, yet fully felt
Connected to our God
Who conquered death to give us new birth
Connected
Forever
One day face-to-face
In a new heaven and earth.
No longer counting minutes
Unaware of time
Praising Him who reigns on High
Him who is Divine.

***

GOD VALUES ME

God values me
He values my friend too
And the stranger on the street
He calls by name. He says, "I love you."
If I'm to become like Him
I must put aside
My quickness to judge
My inflated pride.
My jealous tendencies
Must be put aside
If I'm to value you
For whom the Savior died.
If I could learn your name.
And value who you are
If I could pray for you
Without judging from afar
Perhaps you would discover
He also knows your name
You are valued, you are loved
It's why the Savior came.
Perhaps you'd choose the narrow way
Perhaps you'd claim your cross
If I could value and honor you
No matter what the cost.
If I could become like Him
Forsaking sin
You'd find Him, too.
You'd learn from me
That He loves you

Stranger in the street
Clerk in the store
Colleague in the work
And myriads more.
You'd know for sure that He loves you
You'd want Him to be your Savior, too.
If I could . . .
He says, "My child, you can."

***

QUIET

Quick
Uninvited
Interruptions
Eventually
Tamed.
QUIET.
All is still.
I listen.

Learning
In
Silence
To
Erase
Noise
LISTEN.

I hear Him.
Holy
Immense
Majesty.
HIM.

He tenderly speaks special words of love
Heard in silence
When all is still.

***

A HUMBLED HEART

A humbled heart
Is offered
Sorry for the offense
And eager for reconciliation
A humbled heart
Is convicted
Not wishing to be justified
Not wishing to be recognized
A humbled heart
Is broken
Repentant
And waiting
The receiving
The forgiveness
The restoration
Humbled
The only posture
Possible
For reconciliation
Bowing we become
Forgiven.

***

THE IMPORTANCE OF BEING WISE

Wise men walk firm level paths
That takes them to their God
With hearts guarded against evil influence
They are not distracted.
Looking left or right
With confidence they walk
A pathway bathed in light
By Faith they walk, day or night.

Faith shouts and walls fall
Faith stands at river's edge as waters part
Faith sits by dried up streams listening for His call
Faith offers a repentant heart.

Faith bathes in foreign lakes
Faith waits the promised seed
Faith un-scorched by furnace fire
O, such faith we need.

Faith hides two foreign spies
Faith prays in the lion's den
Faith fells a giant tall
Oh, how we need such faithful men.

***

OUR FATHER
WHICH ART IN HEAVEN

Waiting Father...Welcoming
Loving Father.....Sheltering
Wooing Father....Calling
Strong Father......Helping
Calm Father........Soothing
Knowing Father...Teaching
Generous Father...Providing
Faithful Father......Keeping
Guiding Father......Leading
Wise Father.........Speaking
Just Father...........Correcting
Holy Father.........Commanding
Merciful Father.....Saving
Promising Father...Giving

***

A FATHER AND A SON

Two days of conversation
As the donkey's plodded on
Two days of quiet speculation
For a father and his son.

Isaac, a boy
Full of life with mind so keen
Thrilled to be along
Enthralled by all he's seen.

Abraham grown old
Many years he's left behind
His faithful God has led him
His loving God so kind.

Isaac is to be the lamb
Upon the mountain top
Abraham must obey and trust
Until the Lord says stop.

The Lord's ways are not his
He's learned that full well.
Today the Lord will provide
He tells his heart be still.

God promised. God will fulfill.
Isaac is bound upon the altar built
Abraham raises the knife to kill

And suddenly a voice
Affirms his blood will not be spilt.

The journey home for them
Was it short or was it long?
God's provision etched forever in their memories
Could they contain the song
Of his provision
As they journeyed on
Their faith triumphant, made more strong.

How I'd love to know
The words they spoke that day
On the journey homeward
What did each man say?
Jehovah-Jireh God did it.
As He does again and again
God provides the sacrifice
He pays for all our sin.
Two days of conversation
How I wish I'd been along.

THE LORD IS MY SHEPHERD

Shepherded I wander not for I am led.
Shepherded I hunger not for I am fed.
Shepherded I worry not for He is near.
All powerful protector, I will not fear.
Shepherded I'm corrected.
His rod and staff they comfort me.
In green pastures I lie contentedly
Shepherded I'm guided on paths He knows
By quiet streams my soul restored
Faith seeds my Shepherd grows.
Shepherded I choose to follow where He goes.

Bekka Siggelkoe

THE MORNING STAR

The sun rose this morning
Like it does everyday
Highlighting the tree limbs
In a most glorious way.
The darkness had hid
The woods from my view.
When I arrived in the night,
There wasn't a clue
That beautiful scenery
Awaited my eyes
Today
At the height of the morning's sunrise.
Darkness is like that
It shields from our sight
Treasures and surprises
That bring special delight.
Living in darkness
Unaware of the light
Some friends grope their way
Through each endless night
Failing to see
What my eyes have beheld
The Morning Star's glory
All my darkness has quelled.

***

THE FINGER OF GOD

In Exodus 31, verse 18 says, "When the Lord finished speaking to Moses on Mount Sinai, he gave him the two tablets of the Testimony, the tablets of stone inscribed by the finger of God."

The finger of God
Inscribes stone tablets,
Writes in the sand,
And becomes pierced.
He is a communicating God
That desires His kids understand
His goal
His strategy
His plan
His forever love for man.
So He stoops
He writes
He speaks
Insights.
His pointing finger beckons me close to His side,
As He lovingly opens His arms, oh so wide.
While embraced in His strong and powerful clutch
I'm aware that He loves me ever so much.
He speaks, "Sinning child, who can't keep my decree,
My only Son died and hung on a tree."
How then can I fear His finger,
Whether writing, or pointing at me;
The finger He held out
When it was nailed to a tree?

***

A PRAYER

Lord, may the wounds of my life
And the scars that I bear
Be a beacon for others
Of your Fatherly care.

May the journey I've trod
Over painful terrain
Cause others to join
In the joyful refrain.
You are love
Your arms bear us up
You are love
Regardless of what's in our cup
You are love.

May you who began a good work in my heart
Who promised to finish whatever you start
Find me faithfully yielded and doing my part
O Creator of uniquely designed people art.

***

FRIGHTENING GOD OF THUNDER-ING VOICE

I was reading recently in Psalm 29. I was struck by the
   picture the Psalmist paints of God.

O God
Frightening God of thundering voice,
I have difficulty hearing you
Over the noise of
Splintering cedars, skipping Lebanons and quaking
   deserts.
These noises capture my attention and grip my heart with
   fear.
I cannot cry "Glory" over the noise
Of twisting oaks and bark-stripped trees.
I can only tremble mutely before such terrifying sounds as
   these.
O God, King forever
Strengthen me and grant me the peace you promised
In the midst of noises that make me feel afraid
For I so want to shout "Glory" and be heard
Above the din of fearful things that make me deaf to you.

Bekka Siggelkoe

HOLY PLACES

Holy places
Hallowed
Where shoes are discarded and lay forgotten
In the awe of burning bushes
Not burned.

Holy places
Hallowed
Where animals gaze quieted
Curious of feeding troughs
Filled with the BREAD OF LIFE.

Holy places
Hollowed
Where filled fishing nets
Rip and tear
After a whole night of fishing
For fish that weren't there.

Holy places
Hallowed
Where water buckets lay empty
At the feet of the GIVER OF LIVING WATER,
Who quenches thirst forever.

Holy places
Hallowed
Where frightening storms
Are stilled with just a word

From HIM, the CREATOR.

Holy places
Hallowed
Where a dead girl is
Aroused from sleep
By Him who is the AUTHOR OF LIFE.

Holy places
Hollowed
Where a small boy's lunch
Is multiplied
To feed 5000
Until they're satisfied.

Holy places
Hallowed
Where a garment hem
Brings a hemorrhaging woman
Face to face with
the HEALER,
Who heals her.

Holy places
Hallowed
Where seas become pathways
When beckoned by Him
To come, walk on the water.

Holy places
Hollowed
Where stones roll away

To reveal empty tombs
Where the dead can't stay
Dead.

Holy places
Hallowed
Where nail-scarred hands
Build a cooking fire
To feed the guilty ones
Redeemed.

Holy places
Hallowed
Still today
Where you are
There are holy places hollowed.

If we but could see them.

***

NARROW PATH PILGRIMMAGE

Places where the path is narrow
And where few have walked;
This is the path before me still
And with each step I balk.

The "what ifs" scream
In statements loud and clear
I must not listen
For they only feed my fear.

The narrow path offers solitude
And the quietness I need
To hear the whispers of my companion
It is His Words on which I feed.

I do not know what lies ahead
Or where I'll camp tonight
But I have a guide I trust
One who is my Light.

Though I walk in darkness
I'll never walk alone
Though the path is narrow,
It is the path that leads me home.

***

HOWEVER AND BUT

In the Bible I read two words that trouble me
"However" and "but" can change the flow of history.
Naaman was a valiant soldier "but"
King Solomon richest and wisest king, "however"
Two little words-what sorrow they bring.
Two little words forever
Separating what is
From what will be
If we fail to follow God
Faithfully.

***

A GOOD IDEA, BUT NOT A GOD IDEA

I've built shelters, Lord
You didn't want
And never used
I've made plans
And then I prayed
My good ideas were diffused
With hope
While I craved your blessing.

Falling face down
Scared
No, terrified
I hear the sound of your voice
I see your glory displayed
Your good idea may have been a God idea
You said
If only you had prayed before you planned.

Now stand and listen
I will show you a new thing
Something you could not imagine
Or comprehend
Listen and watch as I my kingdom grow
Without shelters made by man
Who do not pray before they plan.

***

IF ONLY YOU HAD SENT ME A NOTE

Lord Jesus
If only you had sent me a note
Written by your dear hand
Something simple
I could understand

If only you had said
Of the beggars I see
This is my friend
Treat him like me.

If only I saw people
The same way as you
I wonder how it would change
The things that I do?

If only you'd sent me
A reminder or two
Would it matter to me?
Would I love them as you?

My child I did!
If you'd read my Word
It will guide you
All your life through.

Forgive me Lord Jesus
It's true in your Word I see

Do unto others as if it were me
Blessed are you if you love even these
Beggars
Prostitutes
Liars and thieves
Colleagues
Partners
Neighbors and enemies
Blessed are you
If you love even these.

Thank you, Lord Jesus for the note that you sent.

***

SOLDIERS WEAVING

One man standing
Against a whole company of soldiers.
Men trained for fighting
Are weaving thorns instead.
Women's work
For macho men now
Kneeling,
Spitting,
Mocking,
And hitting one solitary unarmed man with a club.
What kind of battle is this for brave men turned bullies?

One man standing,
No longer clothed in Roman spittle,
But gloriously crowned and robed
To face again these same men one-by-one
Who are kneeling, but no longer spitting
Who are proclaiming with tongues that once mocked
    Him
This Jesus is indeed King of the Jews.
These same men are waiting with reverence,
No longer fearless,
No longer jesting,
But wondering what will He who holds the scepter
Do to them now?

On that day every knee will bow
And every tongue confess that

Jesus Christ is Lord.

Every knee,
Every tongue,
Of every soldier
In the whole company assigned to participate in His
     scourging.
These soldiers once placed a crown of thorns on His
     head.
Would He now place one on theirs?

Also you and me
One day before the Christ
On bended knee
At the threshold of eternity.
Oh what a glorious day that will be,

To mock Him or to serve Him,
What will it be?

***

THE TOOLS OF SERVANT-HOOD

Servant-hood's tools:
Simple, common, few:
Water
A towel
A basin.

The posture of servant-hood:
Vulnerable
Humble
Lowly
On one's knees.

The act of servant-hood:
Unglamorous
Unappealing
Unpretentious
Washing dirty feet.

Our example of servant-hood:
Jesus who left
His comfortable place at the table
His outer garments
His entitled privileges as Lord.

Jesus took the tools of servant-hood,
Assumed the posture of servant-hood,
And performed an act of servant-hood
To teach us by example

Something everyone can do
All the time
Anywhere
For anyone.

***

WITH HANDS TO THE PLOW

Hurting missionary women
Young and old
Struggle
Lonely
Sometimes afraid.
Designed to be helpmates,
Yet unmarried,
Still they stayed.
With hands to the plow
They labored on,
Certain somehow
Their Father knew
Each heart's desire
Unfulfilled.
They labored
Lonely,
Sometimes afraid.
Serving they inspire,
Because they stayed.

***

THE CROWD AT THE CROSS

I stood at the foot of the cross today in my mind's eye
And watched the faces of people passing by,
The grieving ones who'd come
To bow their knees and cry.
I saw Simon Peter's mother-in-law wishing
There was something she could do.
He had raised her from her sick bed when she was gravely
    ill
She hated to see Him now so still.
And beside her weeping softly
Was the man whose friends had ripped a roof apart
To put him where he could glimpse the Savior's heart.
A parade of people who had personally met the crucified
Soon became a crowd stretching far and wide.
The Gerasene demoniac clothed and in his right mind
Could not grasp the awful horror of mankind.
The woman of Samaria wept with half her town
All recognizing that these thorns were not his rightful
    crown.
There was Nicodemus wishing he'd been brave
And Joseph of Arimathea offering his grave.
The man whose hand was once withered
Shrunk from hammer sounds delivered.
And blind men, some I knew by name
Stood and watched His pain.
I scanned the crowd, could it be the lepers healed who
    cried aloud
And strained to touch His foot as He had once touched
    them?

I wondered if the woman who His hem had found
Was still alive and like the others kneeling on the ground.
Was that the Centurion and his servant bowing low?
I recognized the paralytic who three short years ago
Took up his mat and walked to show
The Pharisees this man Jesus could bestow forgiveness.
Little children clutching their parents' clothes
Had loved this man who welcomed them in droves.
The dead girl now alive and the man from Nain with his
   widowed Mom
Had come unable to believe what the Pharisees had done.
The little boy was there, who'd given up his lunch
He was looking for a Pharisee he could punch.
The deaf were there when the nailing started
And hearing every hammer thud were brokenhearted.
The Syrophoenician woman who had begged for just a
   crumb
Now knelt in disbelief, her nerves all numb.
The boy who had seizured once at Jesus' feet
Could now only gaze in wonder at the man who'd given
   him relief.
Looming straight and tall she stood out from all the rest
Once a bent and crippled woman she now wailed and beat
   upon her breast.
The woman caught in adultery dared to show her face
Unable to comprehend her Savior's
Place upon the cross in such disgrace.
But missing from the tableau in my mind was Judas.
How could he have been so blind
Not to see his treachery
Would lead to this hill of mockery?
But wait, the story isn't done.

For up from the grave Christ will come;
Life will conquer death. The battle will be won.
Jesus lives again, God's dear Son.
From my place in history
I see what these ones could not see
For their perceived place of hopelessness and misery
Was really just the launching pad of victory.
One day they'll bow again,
This hurting throng,
Before the Living Christ
They'll sing the triumph song
And dance with joy,
For not only did He make them whole
But by dying on the cross
He sanctified their soul.
I'll be there, too, that day He comes again
Joining the throng of witnesses saved from sin
Rejoicing all together we'll praise the Lord of men.

***

HIDDEN BLOOMS

Hidden blooms
Unseen
Bloom anyway.

***

SKILLED ONES

God calls
All the skilled among us
To come.
Shall not all rise
To respond to the call?
Made in His image
Is there anyone among us
Who is not skilled at all?
Made in His image,
Creative like Him,
Can you not hear him calling,
Has your hearing gone dim?
Made in His image, you must stand to your feet.
Skilled one respond;
Don't stay in your seat.
You've been given gifts unique as the rest.
Respond to God's calling and give Him your best.

Bekka Siggelkoe

HARVESTING

A fruitful life
Focused on the Father
Attentive
Alert
Unenticed by worldly longing
Unencumbered by worldly goods
Unworried
Unhurried
At peace
Serene
Welcoming
Secure
A fruitful life
Aware
Of hearts prepared for harvest.

***

GRACIOUS LORD

A child is born,
The product of adultery,
The motive for murder
Yet he is loved, cried over and wept for.
He is an unnamed child
Born to David and Bathsheba
And struck ill by God.
As long as the child lives
Hope burns in David's repentant heart.
It is a hope that does not die with the child.
Out of the ash heap of remorse and grief
A new seed begins to form.
God's redemptive love is revealed
In another child
Later born to David and Bathsheba.
This child named Solomon
Is loved and adored, too.
How gracious is our Lord?
His love is underscored
While His mercy is outpoured.

***

RAISIN CAKES
Based on Hosea 3:1

A wooing God
Who loves His child
Calls again and again,
But running merrily with laughter on her lips
His child ignores the call.
The lure of raisin cakes in yonder stall
Consumes the child who skips
Away from God.
The call goes unanswered.
The temporary pleasure of raisin cakes
Is the stronger desire.
The eternal Presence who satisfies fully
Always calls us higher.
Raisin cakes. How can it be
I substituted raisin cakes for Thee?

***

COMMANDMENTS
Based on I Samuel 15

"Completely destroy" was what God said to Saul
"Completely" should have covered it all.
But the Saul spared the king and the best of the flocks
What was Saul thinking? It's Jehovah he mocks.
Why spare the King of Agag, his sheep and his goats?
"It's obedience God loves," Samuel notes.
Though he was victor in a battle hard-fought,
He succumbed to temptation. With stolen goods he was
     caught.
God loves obedience more than unblemished sheep,
Therefore, I'll strive His commandments to keep.

***

THE PEOPLE WATCHER

Jesus, the people-watcher,
Noticed
A poor widow.
His face lights up.
He grins
And then laughs delightedly.
"Look, look," He points excitedly,
"That widow has given
All she has to the temple treasury."
Jesus, the people-watcher,
Noticed.
What does He see
When He watches me?
I wonder.

***

PRAYER FOR A CENTURION

The carpenter nailed the wood to build a table or chair.
The centurion nailed the carpenter to crucify Him.
Nails of the carpenter's trade become tools of blessing by
    what is made.
Nails of the centurion's profession become tools of
    condemnation.
The carpenter creating
The centurion condemning
The carpenter nailed by the centurion nailing.
The carpenter praying
The centurion slaying
The carpenter making a way to life
The centurion murdering to death
The carpenter hanging on the tree
The centurion dropping to his knee
The carpenter proclaims it is finished.
The centurion exclaims, "Surely this must be the Son of
    God."
The carpenter nailed by the centurion nailing the
    crucified.
Thus, the carpenter Jesus died.

***

ADULTERER

Based on John 8

Woman,
Daughter,
Mother,
Wife.

Woman
When did you begin
To walk the path of sin?
How were you led astray?
Why did you disobey?
The Law of Moses clear and true,
"Thou shalt not commit adultery",
Was God's law for you.

Daughter,
Was your father kind and brave?
Did he teach you, love you, rave
About your beauty?
Were you his pride and joy,
Or did he rather wish you had been a boy?

Mother,
Bearer of children born in pain
Without love to sustain
Through the daily chores
Of rearing daughters and sons.
A dalliance here and there.

229

Who's going to care
If you have a little fun?

Wife,
Submitting, yet not getting
From a husband on the run,
Is caught in the act
With another mother's son.
How could you?
Why would you?
No denying what you've done.

You are caught
Condemned
Brought
Before the Son of Man.
The accusers gather stones
You sense you're just a pawn
You wait
You watch
Your hope is long gone.

Finally in shock and disbelief
You hear the stones they hold clatter
As they're dropped to the ground.
Your accusers all leave,
Not making a sound.
Then slowly He turns around.

Woman,
Daughter
Mother

Wife
His words are softly spoken,
He's offering you life.

Bekka Siggelkoe

STONES?

I hold out my hands palms up
Ready to receive.
The heaviness I feel
As my fingers close around
God's answer confuses me.
Are these not stones, Lord?
How can this be bread for me?

Vengeance is mine
I will repay
Call upon me
I am just
All wrongs will one day
Be made right
All deeds will be exposed to Light.

Wait, wait, trust and pray
Vengeance is mine
I will repay
I Am just.

I reign supreme.
I Am God
There is none higher than Me
I, the Lord God Almighty,
Reign sovereignly.
Wait, wait, my kingdom is coming
I'll have my way.

I Am. I hear you pray.

Your daily bread
Your just reward.
I, Jehovah God
Your Sovereign Lord.
Give,
Judge,
Love,
You have my Word.
This that feels like stone IS bread.
Trust me, taste and see.
"I Am," God said.

***

TIMELESS ONE

O Timeless One
You chose to be confined
To the limitations
Of minutes,
Hours,
Days.
To the marking-off of time.
How timeless is that?

O Eternal One
Who is I Am.
You chose to take on flesh
So you could live and die.
The One who is and was and is to come
Is lifted high on wooden beams.
How eternal is that?

O Holy One
Who knew no sin.
You chose to bear my evil acts
To go to hell for me.
You died in my place
As your Father turned His back.
How sinless is that?

O Loving One
Loving unconditionally
You chose to give me freedom
You did it all

With no strings attached.
Now I choose
To love you back
Or not.
How loving is that?

***

A THOUSAND YEARS

Oh, God to whom a thousand years is but a day
Why did you send Jesus to earth for so short a stay?
Thirty-three were the sum of His years
Only three spent in ministry along with His peers.
Does it not pose a mystery, or result in great awe
That we still worship Jesus, or know Him at all?

***

WHO IS LIKE YOU?
Based on Deut. 33

Who is like you
A people saved by the Lord?
He is your shield
Your helper
Your glorious sword.
He rides on the heavens
On the clouds He comes
With majesty.
The Eternal One.
He's your refuge
Your warrior strong
On the clouds He comes
Saving those who belong.
He's your shield
Your helper
Your glorious sword
He is God Almighty
Majestic Lord
On the clouds He comes
With majesty
The Eternal One
To set me free.

Bekka Sigglekoe

DRIED UP BROOKS

By the brook Elijah sat deep in thought
Its thirst-quenching waters had satisfied the drought.
Alone he pondered what God had taught.
But as time passed by
The waters ceased.
No gurgling spring
No refreshing spray
The brook just dried up one day.

Elijah stayed and waited
For the voice of His Lord
He trusted not in the gift
It was the Giver he adored.

There must be some other stream
And Jehovah Jireh knows just where
I'll drink refreshed and satisfied
If I let Him lead me there.

By dried up brooks
I've sat also.
Impatiently I waited
Until the Lord said, "Go."

"Go to a widow,
To a mother lost in grief,
To a child abused,
To a dying thief.

Go, I've got things for you to do
Once you've learned at dried-up streams
I'll show you other things
Beyond what you could dream.

Go, child, I'll lead the way.
Dried-up brooks are not the end of things;
They're just a place to temporarily stay
Until you learn to trust the Giver
More than the gift He brings."

***

JESUS KNEELING

He knelt
His position was vulnerable but non-threatening
While angry men clutched stones, waiting.
Jesus began writing on the ground, what?
We'll never know the words
The Word wrote that day.
But obediently one-by-one each angry man turned away
From Jesus kneeling.

His power was not in posture
Nor in voice raised.
He commanded quietly
As onlookers gazed.

This man called Jesus
With authority profound
Could command grown men
While writing on the ground.

Kneeling Jesus,
Look into my heart I pray.
Help me not to gather stones
As I journey through today.

***

CLINGING

I'm clinging to the Savior
Whose arms I cannot feel
I'm listening to the silence
While at the cross I kneel.

The darkness presses close
The silence crowds me too
Yet clinging ever tighter
I hunger for a word from you.

Precious Savior
Your joy I long to know
Though the cross is heavy
Yet where you go, I'll go.

At the cross I kneel
Clinging to the Savior
Whose arms I cannot feel
Listening to the silence
To words I cannot hear
Still I'm clinging to the Savior
Who promised to be near.

**

FRESH WORDS

Fresh words
Found in fresh wounds
From the living of today
In such a way
As to cling to the vine.
New songs,
New wine,
I am His and He is mine.
Nothing stale,
Nothing lost,
Mindful always of the cost.
His life for mine.
Mine lived to the full,
Fresh and vibrant,
Never dull.
Clinging,
Singing,
Silent,
Held,
His life for mine,
My fears are quelled.
I can feed others from what He feeds me.
Fresh word He speaks,
New things I see,
When I sit at His feet daily.

***

QUIETLY CONNECTING

Connecting
God and me.

Resting.
I open my eyes to see
He's been working,
Transforming me.

Listening.
I sit alone quietly
With ears attuned
I hear His voice only.

The stillness hugs me and I smile.
Waiting.
The Sabbath soothes and cleanses.
In the deeper reaches foreign to my consciousness
Healing happens
Though I rarely know it until later.
The quiet place,
My refuge.
The stillness,
My cloak.

I hear His voice welcoming and full of love.
I could stay here forever in this place of peace.
I feel Him erase
All the worry lines that etch my face.

All strivings cease and in their place
He pours in me His grace.

But nipping at the borders
Ruthlessly in an effort to distract
Busyness calls to me,
"Don't desert the task. There's work to do, you shirker.
Don't relax."
It is an effort to block out the noise
But the silence beckons softly
So I stay,
Refusing to allow busyness to win this day.
God calls. I will obey.

***

HE WALKS WITH ME

I walk among miracles.
Some I recognize.
Most I don't see.
The Emmanuel God
Visible here
Invisible there
Walks with me.

Sometimes it's the fragrance of His love
That captures my attention,
So I look more carefully.
Sometimes it's a faint whisper heard
Above the din as He calls to me.
Sometimes it's the pressure of His arm's embrace
That causes me to trace
His outline at my side.

Through every circumstance,
Regardless of its kind,
I find
He's there
Working with tender care,
Heeding my every prayer
Completing what He began in me when I was ten.

Daily I walk among miracles.
He catches my eye,

Wanting to see if I'm noticing
Or merely passing by.

I walk among miracles.
Some I recognize
Most I don't even see.

But thankfully, He walks with me
Whether I notice Him or not.

***

LIVING IN BETWEEN

It's hard to live our lives in-between.
To long for rewards unseen,
Only promised,
Not yet claimed,
Only imagined,
Not yet named.
In between living,
Restless,
Insecure;
Afraid.
I wonder if God can do what He said.
If only we had stayed
Where things were certain,
Settled,
Routine.
There'd be no longing
For things not seen,
No sense of living in between.

***

CAPTURED

I knew some friends captured and held
By men who knew not love.
They walked the jungle trails hands tied
Stumbling, bruised and blistered
Sore, looking always up above,
They walked some days unsure.
Was it the path of death
They walked today?
No matter, death or life,
Their Savior knew the way.
They cried tears,
Each one caught and stored
In jars and bottles
Held by hands nail-scarred.
They prayed aloud and silently
As hate hissed and soared
With fangs unfurled.
How often it had bitten deep
Cascading tears and thwarting sleep.
Sick and tired, discouraged and abused,
They walked and talked together
Occasionally confused.
Where was the God they loved,
All the miles they trod?
Each day they searched
To see the face of God.
And He was there.
Present.

Helpful.
Serene.
The Lord of Lords
And King of Kings
No eye hath seen.

But He was there.
They knew it well.
The God they loved and feared,
What stories they would tell.
His love was grand
Upsetting all the plans of evil man
Hands tied, heads bowed
They paused each day and said aloud,

"You are Sovereign Lord of love
Supreme
High and lifted up.
Nothing is impossible.
You say the Word
And it is done.
We dare to come.
Your Holy place is open,
Opened by the Son.
We bow in reverence,
Bow in fear.
We dare to ask,
Please draw near
And walk with us.
This path that is our lot,
Grant us grace to bear the ropes
Until you untie the knot.

Dare we ask,
Please walk with us.
We bow in reverence
And in fear.
In you O God Majestic One we trust.
As step-by-step
We see the pathway clear.
Awed,
We are grateful
You are here."

***

WAITING, WATCHING, WORSHIPPING

Sheep on a hillside
Watched by shepherds in a tower.
Sheep without spot or blemish.
Sacrificial lambs without power.
WAITING.

Post Crucifixion. Pre-resurrection.
The disciples are locked in the Upper Room.
Afraid. Despairing.
Facing certain doom.
WAITING.

In the quietness of the night,
The angel parts heaven's curtain
With a message so profound,
The shepherds were uncertain.
WATCHING.

An empty cross.
A stone-covered tomb.
Bored soldiers yawn
Weeping women stumble in the dawn.
WATCHING.

A sheep has left His place on high.
The Savior came to a stable bare.
Like a newborn lamb, meekly cradled, helpless small.

They look at Him with awe and bow.
WORSHIPPING.

Jesus is alive.
With alarm and surprise,
They touch His feet, seek His eyes.
The Savior is alive.
They look at Him with awe and bow.
WORSHIPPING.

And so today we wait, watch and worship too. He's
    coming again. I'm eager to see His face. Aren't you?

ALONE TIMES
Based on Genesis 32:22-32

Alone times
Are opportune times
For wrestling.
Alone at night encounters
With God.
Times for overcoming or being overcome.
Life-changing encounters we limp away from,
Feeling blessed, though crippled.
Before daybreak with fundamental character flaws
      exposed,
We become more human,
More open,
Less fearful,
More whole.
Aware that God's mercy is
Not gentle,
Not fragile,
Not limited.
That God's blessing is His mercy.
It comes not from grabbing
But from clinging.
We face a new dawn unafraid, not alone,
Forever changed,
Forever blessed.

***

SHATTERED AND BROKEN

She sat
Frayed like rope fibers coming apart.
I listened.
Slowly over time
Life stresses had fractured her heart,
And the story pieces being scattered before me
Would perhaps be the start
Of the mending required for this broken heart.

Though she had known of Him
The One who designed her small frame,
And though she once loved Him
And exalted His name,
She now lived for herself only,
Not caring that He came.

Though she remembered the lessons from youth,
And the Sunday School teacher who taught her the truth,
She had grown beyond those childish things.
Or so she said, as she fingered her rings.

I see her
Shattered and broken with nowhere to turn.
My heart wants to tell her
Some truths that I've learned.
But watching her cry,
I know the timing's not right.

For words cannot yet
Turn her darkness to light.

I wait silently
As the minutes tick by.
Thankful to the Savior
Who collects each tear from her eye.

I feel Him near me
And wonder, does she feel Him too?
If only she could hear Him,
Tell her what's true.

He's the One
Who can make the wrongs right.
He's the One
Who can turn darkness to light.
He's the One
Lover of her soul.
He's the One
Who can again make her whole.

***

GOD'S CHARACTER

Bearing the yoke alone
Silently
In grief
I wait.
The pouring out of hope
And ceaseless loving kindness.
I'm a sinner
Not daring to complain
To the holy God
Called Love,
The pursuing God
Called Omnipotent,
The omniscient God
Called wise.
Great is His faithfulness.
The Hope Restorer reigns supreme.
His goodness
Clothes me with mercy.
Every new tomorrow
I bravely face
Because He is Omnipresent.

***

HIS AROMA

I want to smell of Jesus
As I journey on my way
I want to leave the scent of Him
On all I do and say.

I want to smell of Jesus
To perfume the air around me
To leave others wondering
What this smell might be.

I want to smell of Jesus,
Leave His fragrance where I go
I want to draw others to Him
Who will smell of Him also.

I want to smell of Jesus
The scent distinctly His
I want to leave others asking
Whose aroma is this?

***

UNFORGIVENESS

My question took her back
And I saw it in her eyes
The happy bride unafraid
Unaware that one day lies
Would destroy the dreams she'd made.
Her mate's betrayal act by act
Each became a brick
She used to build a wall
Now impenetrably thick.
The barbed wire scar marks
Ripped apart her heart
Bleeding out the love it held
At her wedded start.
Unforgiveness ravaged
Wrinkle lines across her face.
And when I offered it,
She refused the cup of grace.
With sadness
I watched her walk away
Her mate had wronged her
Was all she had to say.
I saw her turn the key
To lock her heart up tight
And I wept with certainty
Two wrongs never make a right.

Diana Stuhr

HIDE AND SEEK

Sometimes the inside of me doesn't match the outside.
The masks and shields I design
Are meant to cover up reality.
You'll look and never find who I really am.
As I grow older, the masks and shields change.
We call it maturity.
Yet I merely rearrange the colors, the shapes.
I gather more masks, more shields
As subtleness becomes an art undeveloped in children
Who are fresh from God until they learn their part
In the game of hide and seek.
We play all through our life.
We rarely get found and we rarely find
In our seeking another kind of fresh-from-God feeling
That liberates.
With masks lowered, shields toppled, we see God,
Maker of Mankind.
No masks or shields clutter His creative space.
Where, with skill and uniqueness He makes a human
    face.
A new creation unmasked.
If we, but could erase the hidden things and be honest
    with each other,
What a different world this would be.
If only I could find you and you could find me.
1-2-3, ready or not, here I come.

***

THE PERFUMER
Based onLuke 7.

So many men's fingers have run through her hair
Dare
She use it to dry his oiled feet?
Surely He knows
How her life story goes
All her feelings of utter defeat?
All that she's done.
All the places she's run.
Her heart is bowed down.
She kneels on the ground.
While the oil caresses His feet.
Now dried with her hair
Her task is complete.
How did she dare?
Why did she come?
A sinner with blackened heart bowed
Is searching to find the way home
If only allowed.
What will He say?
What will He do?
She's messed up her life.
The stories are true.
Unworthy,
Unwanted,
Unloved,
Unable to move.

She waits not daring to breathe.
What will the Savior do?

He'll cleanse her heart
As heaven's portals He'll part.
He'll shower His grace
As He takes her place
Drinking God's cup of wrath
He'll open the path
To her heavenly home
And invite her there
Where they can both share
A forever.
Together.
The spiller of fragrance,
The spiller of blood
Both look to the Father
Ultimate spiller of love.

***

THE WELCOMING JESUS

Matthew 26:29 says, "I tell you, I will not drink of this
fruit of the vine from now on until that day when I
drink it anew with you in my Father's kingdom."

I see Jesus waiting
With wine glass in hand
Ready to toast
My arrival home.
Maybe it will be at the wedding feast of the lamb
When all His Bride is gathered
That He'll finally raise His glass and toast His children
Naming them one by one
And after all are named
He'll drink anew the fruit of the vine just like He
promised.
I see Jesus waiting to give the benediction
The ending and beginning prayer.
"To life," He may shout.
To life forever basking in His glory.
The One and Only Son is looking forward to my coming.
He's waiting for me,
With wine glass in hand.

***

AUTHOR

Author of this chapter of my life
And every chapter past
Write on the pages what you will
Grow faith in me to last
All future chapters you design
Author and Lord of time.
As the tide rolls out
Leaving the shoreline bare
Remind me of your care
Help me contentment find
Author and Lord of time.
Grow faith in me to last
All future chapters you design
Author and Lord of time.

***

THE ANCHOR

You are the anchor
Lord of my soul
You speak to the waves
You have Sovereign control.
You are the anchor
That steadies my boat
You capture the winds
You keep me afloat.
You are the anchor
King of my life
You grant me peace
In the midst of my strife.
You are the anchor
I know what to do
Powerful Savior
I'll cling only to you.
You are the anchor
I'm safe and secure
You are the anchor
My harbor is sure.

***

CARRIED AND LOVED

Carried and loved
Sheltered and held
My Savior's nearness
All my fears quelled.

Happy and carefree
Peaceful and calm
My Savior's comfort
The heart of my Psalm.

Saved and forgiven
Freed from all wrong
His resurrection
The theme of my song.

Looking to heaven
My sins erased
My Father's welcome
The smile on His face.

***

A DAUGHTER'S QUESTIONS

When did you stop loving, Mother?
When was the fire of compassion choked forever
And banished from your heart?
You were loved.
I see it in my father's eyes
In photos as he looks at you.
Did you love him back?

Did you know joy when you first held me in your arms?
Did you hug me close with a smile on your face?
Or was I a burden, a responsibility to tie you down
And keep you home? A blot you wished you could erase?

Have you no capacity for love?
Are there no empty places left in your bitter burdened
        heart
Where bits of love can bud and blossom and become
A flower so exquisite
So uniquely
You?
For expressing and receiving love is what we're meant to
        do.

Why is it always someone else's fault?
Why can't you own your own mistakes?
When did you kill your conscience?
Do you even know it's gone?
What kind of song do bitterness and loneliness sing to you

In the darkest hours of the night?
Are there embers smoldering yet,
A tiny spark to be ignited once again,
A facing of the wrong,
A stirring of regret,
A realization it's not too late?
Joy and love He offers you.
What will you do? What will you choose?

***

THE GOD WHO BRINGS OUT

I am the Lord God who brings you out
Of Egypt
Of the fiery furnace
Of the lion's den
Of indebtedness
Of low self-esteem
Of loneliness
Of grief
I'm the God who brings you out.
Places of bondage can be left behind.

He's bringing out the captives
Who will join the throng?
He's bringing out the captives
Will you come along?

Will you and you and you be brought out?
He's calling to the schemer, "Let my people go."
Will you be brought out?
Will you go?

Bekka Siggelkoe

WINTER, COLD AND GRAY
Based on John 10:22-42

It was winter, cold and gray.
Accusations hurled about
Like blizzard snow and they,
The ones who want to know
Shout, "Are you the Christ?
Say plainly it is so".
The Christ, He lifts His gaze
To realms on high
And silently He prays,
"For these my Father
I came to die,
These helpless ones
Now asking why.
I tell them you and I are one,
The Father and the Son."
But each accuser grabs a stone
And strikes a pose.
Blasphemy they shout as one.
And quickly their anger grows
While I, the Christ, turn away and sadly go.
And they,
The ones who want to know
Can only drop their stone
Surprised they are alone,
In the winter cold and gray.

***

THE DEAD TREE

Stark and bare it caught my eye;
A bush all but dead stretching empty branches to the sky.
But plain to see,
Three blooms bright red
Stuck out in contrast
To what looked dead.

My life seems like that tree
Dead branches wrinkled old and bare
Leave me sad and sorry.
But a green leaf here and there
Tell the truer story.

The bush is not dead;
Just dormant now.
Another season it will radiant be.
Please, Lord, preserve the bud and one day blossom all of
    me.

***

MARY'S SONG

Mary
Pregnant
Singing
No worries plague her believing heart.
God is mindful of her and she of him.
The Mighty One
She remembers great things He has done.
For her, He'll do His part.

She hums the song,
As a smile lights up her face.
God will make a way.
She welcomes the mantle of disgrace.
For her, the stigma He'll erase.
He'll call to Joseph and state her case.
God will make a way; a way of grace.

Her feet pick up the rhythm
Tapping out the beat.
The seed of Messiah is planted in her womb.
A mother's dreams are complete
The song cascades around the room.
A song of joy, not of defeat.
No sense of dread or doom.
No cross, no garden tomb,

The song is laughter
Rippling through the air

Mary knows that God is there.
His peace a soothing balm,
Her heart a sea of calm
She surrenders to His care.

***

WILL HE SPEAK?

Watchfully, waiting, silently
I sit in solitude listening attentively
And asking in my heart, "Will He speak?"
Will the silence be broken
By the Word Maker whose word
Created worlds, suns, moons, stars and me?
Embracing the silence
And gathering it around me like a shroud,
I am cocooned by its safety.
Harsh words aren't allowed
In this arena of chosen silence
Where I sit alone with my thoughts and questions
Waiting for the One with answers to speak.
I welcome His words
For they quiet my heart
And remind me of His love,
Which is unconditional and everlasting.
I am rewarded and the waiting is not long.
I hear Him speak my name, soft, yet strong.
When God says, "Diana"
I hear delight in His voice.
When God says, "Diana"
I know I'm His choice.
When God says, "Diana"
I humbly obey.
When God says, "Diana"
All fears melt away.
When God says, "Diana"

I know it will all be OK.
His eyes lock with mine
Tender and sweet.
I'm thankful I waited
Certain He'd speak.
When God says, "Diana"
A smile lights up His face.
When God says, "Diana"
I invite His embrace.

***

STILLNESS

There is stillness.
I'm waiting
Listening
For the God who is longing
To be gracious
To speak.
Silent tears
Depicting anguish
Are gently brushed away.
The unspoken cry
Is heard by a listening God
Longing to be gracious.
His voice a whisper
Soft
Soft.
The quieted one hears clearly His Word,
"This is the way
Walk ye in it."
The stillness is broken
By the One who speaks
A whisper that is
Hushed in tones
Only the quieted one can hear.
She is conscious now of Him who is near
To all who cry silently
He is a very present help.
He speaks.

Made in the USA